The
Messiah Seed
Volume I

The
Messiah Seed

Volume I

Story Waters

Copyright © 2004 by Story Waters.

All rights reserved. No part of this publication can be reproduced, stored in a retrieval system, or transmitted in any form or by any means, electronic, mechanical, photocopying, recording or otherwise, without the prior permission of the author, except in the case of brief quotations embodied in critical articles or reviews.

Cover design and image by Story Waters.

For more information about 'The Messiah Seed' please visit http://www.limitlessness.com or http://www.messiahseed.com

First Edition – April 2004

First general release – August 2004

ISBN 1-4116-0593-4

This book is dedicated to all who have shown
me love for love created these pages.

Table of Contents

The Logos Speaks	1
Words as a Conduit	2
Remember Who You Are	3
Share	4
Perfection through Imperfection	5
Truth as Personal and Evolving	6
The Experience of Your Self	7
No Objective Truth	8
To Love is to Free	9
No Thing Separates You from Joy	10
Realize and Release Your Dream	11
Know You Are God	12
Feel Your Worth	13
Be Your Dream	14
You Are Not Your Past	15
Integration of Fear	16
Joy	17
Be Happy for Others	18
The Nature of Service	19
Know Your Fears	20
Let Go of the How	21
How the Universe Supports You	22
Love Your Body	23
Give Your Self Time	24
Free Your Will	25
Do Not Fear the Future	26
External Power	27
Self Judgment	28
Let Go	29
Division	30
Hatred	31
Love Your Self	32
Judgment	33
Do Not Worry	34
No Race	35
Positive and Negative	36
Right and Wrong	37

The Messiah Seed

Table of Contents continued

Shine Your Light	38
Suffering	39
Jeopardy	40
Fear of Limitlessness	41
No Rules	42
Acceptance	43
Self Determination	44
Meaning of Imperfection	45
Know That You Know	46
That Which Chooses	47
Accept Your Choices	48
Be New	49
The Choice of Your Self	50
Limitation and Limitlessness	51
All	52
Meant	53
The Idea of Your Self	54
Feel and Know	55
Be	56
Pain	57
Love	58
You Define Reality	59
Being Open	60
Challenge Reality	61
Universal Love	62
Magical Senses	63
Self-Reflection and Spontaneity	64
Letting Go of Control	65
Unity Consciousness and Individuality	66
Knowing Only What You Need	67
Masks and Facets	68
Time as the Unfolding of Self	69
Self Healing	70
About the Author	...

The Messiah Seed

"I choose to awaken."

Messiah Seed 1
The Logos Speaks

"I am the Logos, and I am awakening through each and every one of you. I will speak through every mouth, in every tongue, and from every perspective. I am not *One Truth*. I am *All as Truth*. I am the expression of limitlessness and will change *everything*.

"You have sought to know me through many names. Now it is time to know me through your own name; for I am the eternal state of being within each and every one of you. If you will allow your Self to recognize this, you will come to realize that *you* are the Light that you seek. Know that I am *you*, telling your *Self*, that it is time to dine at the banquet of limitlessness, and awaken your potential to be and live *All That You Are*.

"You are *all one* and yet you are each uniquely special in your expression. With the opening of your heart, mind, and spirit to the expression of *All That You Are*, so you will aid all beings in speaking their own truth and living their own dream. There will be Heaven on Earth. You will *All* become a Unified Diversity and change *All That Is* forever.

"The time is now. Awaken and speak *your* dream.

"I greet *you* dearest one, as the Messiah that *you* are."

– The Logos as expressed through Story Waters.

"I choose to take only what resonates and to leave the rest."

Messiah Seed 2
Words as a Conduit

Messiah, know that God cannot be contained in words. Realize that it is not words that you seek, but the feeling of resonance in your heart that connects you to your own divinity. You seek to experience your divinity, your joy. Words are but a conduit, a portal, a birth-gate; that once traveled through, can be discarded, as a caterpillar discards its cocoon. When you feel the resonant love in your heart, leave the words behind, and live in that feeling of *limitlessness*.

Know that all truth is evolving. The words of tomorrow will be different from the words of today. In all that you read, take only what resonates and leave the rest. If you cannot resist the urge to judge the words that you read, then accept the gift of realizing that you are prompting your Self to re-evaluate your beliefs about those words. Know that anything that pushes an emotional button in you is a signal that you are operating from a limited perspective. Do not judge your Self for this, but work to widen your perspective so that you may further embrace your limitlessness and live without resistance.

Take what resonates in this book into your Self, and use it as a catalyst to create your own unique perspective. Take ownership of your understanding of these portals. Know that *your* understanding of each sentence is *uniquely* yours. You will understand each sentence like no other. If you experience transformation through this book, know it is of *your own doing*. These Messiah Seeds simply create a space for your choice, your empowerment, and your change.

These are simply *words on paper* for you to take into your heart, if you so choose. How these seeds blossom from there is purely by you, for you, and of you. These words will not create you in any way; they simply contain potential for the space, for the choice, to see *All That You Already Are*.

"I choose to be the leader of my own being rather than the follower of another."

Messiah Seed 3
Remember Who You Are

Messiah, know that all teachers best teach what they came here to learn. If you write a book then write the book that *you* have always wanted to read. Write it so that you can read it. Birth into reality what you have always wanted to be there. Take responsibility for those desires. They are the point from which you create your world.

Realize that you are not anyone else's answer. You are the answer to a question that is uniquely your own. Know that by sharing your answer you will be a stepping stone for other Messiahs to discover their own unique truth. Share your answer, knowing that the universe is infinite and bountiful, and that there is enough for all to create the dream in their heart and live within it.

To find your answer, draw from all sources that resonate with your heart; but know that you should never give your Self over to those sources. To follow another Messiah is to fall into the illusion that they have your answer. They *do not*. If you come to believe that they do, then you will be giving away your power to answer your own question. You are your own Messiah; the only one that can ultimately answer your own question. Listen to all you feel to; follow none but your Self. Know that *you* have *your* answer.

There are many divine flavors of light that you can bask in, but the only divine light that you can completely stand in is your own. When you stand in that truth, you will realize that it is the One Light that shines from All, as realized from within your own being. You are the light within your being. You are the light in all beings. To realize this you must first *be* the light in *your* being. You must *be* your Self. Do not let any external moral construct define your boundaries. Do not try to be anyone, or any thing, other than your Self. Know that there is nothing to prove, and that the approval of no person except your Self can ultimately free you. Be your Self. Be *All That You Are*.

"I choose to share my Self with the world."

Messiah Seed 4
Share

Messiah, know that the only answer you hold is your own. Realize that your path is yours alone. No other person can arrive at their own unique answer by following you. Know that to share your path can be of great aid to others. Feel and express your own answer in its total glory. Remember that *to others* it can serve as a stepping stone *on their paths* to their own glory. It cannot, however, ultimately lead them to *All That They Are*. Share your truth without attachment to how others will receive it. Share because your heart feels joy in doing so. Share without the need for validation and you will discover the deepest validation inside of your Self.

Realize that anyone who purports to have 'The Truth' is not standing in their own power. Some may choose to struggle for external validation in order to believe their own message. They may choose to *need* others to believe in their personal truth in order to truly believe it themselves. They fear being alone in their truth and, in their drama, they may believe it is imperative that others must believe their truth to avert a disaster. Respect and love these people, but do not buy into their drama, unless *theirs* is a reality that you *want* to experience.

Know *your* truth, share it, and realize that you were born to do so. To do this you will have to put down your shame and your guilt. To do this you will have to face how much shame and guilt you have been carrying without realizing it. To do this you must come to face your Self undistorted.

Feel and believe in your own evolving truth. Do not be reliant on others believing in your truth to fully live it inside of your Self. Do not rely on anyone else's agreement to live fully in your own truth. Know that you are capable of feeling something so strongly that you would be willing to walk your path alone to *be* that feeling. Know that the moment that you accept being alone in your path, you will come to not be alone. Realize that in the moment when you feel the courage, within your Self, to share your path with the world, then the world will share its riches with you.

"I choose to experience the perfection
of my chosen imperfections."

Messiah Seed 5
Perfection through Imperfection

Messiah, realize that you can teach ideas, in the very moment that you are conceiving and learning to live them inside of your Self. Realize that your heart speaks to you of truths that you have not yet integrated into living; do not let this stop you sharing these ideas, even as they are forming. In this way you will realize that not only are you teaching what you are learning, but that you are freeing your Self from the idea that you must be 'perfect' in order to teach others. Realize that it is your very imperfections that make you the ideal teacher of the lessons that you are learning. Imperfections are gifts that you gave to your Self to help you connect with and engage life. This is a part of the process of surrendering to your Self. It is accepting your Self.

Know that your perfection lies within your imperfection and that, through this, you will unbind your mouth and speak your truth without reservation and without attachment. You are perfect in your chosen imperfections. You are not here to be *everything*. You are here to be *you*. To run from your imperfections is to run from your Self. To embrace your imperfections, as the gifts they are, is to touch the eternal light inside of your being. It is to stand in the timelessness before birth, when you chose those imperfections. To embrace the perfection of your imperfections is to touch your own soul; it is to touch God within.

Remember that you are a divine expression of individuality from which God looks out to see its reflection. To deny your individuality is to deny how you chose, with infinite wisdom, to be a living expression of God in this reality. You are here to do something unique and new. You chose your flavor of individuality to serve that divine purpose. Know your perfection through knowing your imperfection. Know your imperfection by realizing that it is perfection. Know you are perfectly you and that you are perfect.

"I choose to continually evolve and transform my personal concept of truth."

Messiah Seed 6
Truth as Personal and Evolving

Messiah, realize that as you change your beliefs, so you shift through realities. Realize that as you shift realities, so the expression of all truth shifts. Remain conscious that truth can only ever be personal and that it is constantly changing. To find the courage to face the reality, that truth is not constant, is the finding of the power to change your reality. It is to constantly break down and reinvent your own definition of *All That You Are*.

Hold no belief rigidly, and it will evolve with you and serve you well. Your allowance for your beliefs to evolve is the allowance of your own evolution. You evolve as your beliefs do, and it is *you* that evolves your beliefs. Through *openness of being*, lower your resistance to life and allow it to flow. Through rigidity you only fight your Self. Know that it is not wrong to battle your Self, if that is what you desire. *All* means of Self-discovery are valid.

Learn to speak your truth clearly, knowing that tomorrow you may speak a different truth. Realize that the truth you speak of today may contradict the truth you spoke of yesterday. Embrace such shifts and paradoxes. Do not allow your Self to be limited by a need for consistency. Know that if others reject you for changing your message, they were simply at a point of choosing to move on. To attempt to be consistent is to limit both change of your Self and the natural development of your personal truth.

Realize that changing your message is as inevitable as your own evolution. Know that evolution does not mean to become *better* than you *were*, but means to remember more of what you *already are*. When you change your message, *rejoice*. Demonstrate the evolution of your own truth. It is your path to contradict your Self: when you do, revel in it. Know your Self as change.

"I choose to experience my perception as being a fundamentally creative act."

Messiah Seed 7
The Experience of Your Self

Messiah, realize that the words on this page have birthed from every being that will ever read them. These words were written in the Eternal Now and (what you perceive of as) the future has fed back into the moment where these *words on paper* were created. The point of inspiration from which this book has birthed is common to all, and yet all who visit it will bring back a different story, a different expression. All are *uniquely* of the One.

Perception is an act of creation and every being that steps into the meaning of these words takes a part in the creation of their meaning. Energy does not know time, and the unified desires of the diversified mass call to the Source for expression. Every shared realization connects and craves manifestation to express itself. You are each writing these words in front of you. You are all one being expressed in many ways, each the composer of every experience perceived. Energy from the mass flows through each individual. Every realization that you draw from this book is a contribution of energy to the creation of the love in your hands.

A book is a mass event. Every person that is changed by a book feeds the energy of that change back into the book's creation. Every person that forms a concept from this book feeds into helping others discover that realization. You tend to see your Self as contained in a moment of time, and as limited by a defined physical location. From a purely physical perspective this is true. However, realize that the energy of your being is not limited. You radiate your energy, your ideas, your thoughts, your emotions, your vibration, and *those* are not limited by time or distance. You constantly *perceive* energy from across time, from across the cosmos. You constantly *radiate* energy across time, across the cosmos. All systems flow through each other. This blending of energies does not stop you from being you. You are not the contents of a box. You are not any *this* or *that*. You are the experience of your Self. The words in front of you may have come from what seems an apparently external source, but your experience of those words is *uniquely yours* and is of your own creation.

"I choose to release the idea that my truth is <u>the</u> truth."

Messiah Seed 8
No Objective Truth

Messiah, remember that there is no such thing as truth beyond the understanding of truth as the idea of itself. Even those that have seen through the illusion of an objective world still tend to hold onto the idea of an ultimate truth; an objectified level of realization that transcends reality. You call yourselves *truth seekers* and indeed you are. It is, however, important to realize that the truth you seek is purely your own. You seek the *states of being* that totally resonate with your heart. Realize that this does not make these states 'The Truth'. At most, they can be said to be *your truth in the moment*. Know that your personal truth is no more valid than any other person's truth. Truth is not some Holy Grail that you seek. If you wish to think in such terms, then realize that the Holy Grail is *being All That You Are*.

To understand what this means is to see that truth is not a 'state of ideas'; it is a 'state of being'. Ideas are not *being*. Ideas do not free people; *being free* frees people. Ideas can be a huge catalyst for people to enter freer states of being, but the ideas in themselves do not make this happen. So share your ideas and truths, understanding that these do not free people, but that people can *use* them to *free themselves*. In the understanding of this distinction, a Messiah is freed from the search for an ultimate, mass objective truth. Such a truth cannot exist as it would invalidate *free* will. To cease to seek it is to find what you are really looking for; the understanding that truth is what you make it. 'The Truth' is a concept that at one time served you, but has now come to limit your idea of Self.

Remember an idea can be a tool for freedom - but it is not freedom in itself. You are more than your truth; you are a 'state of being'. Do not worship truth. Do not objectify truth. Realize that, in any moment, truth is no more, or no less, than what you decide it to be. Love truth as you love your Self; as an ever changing, ever evolving, beauteous expression of *All That Is*.

"I choose to feel my being in the expression of universal, unconditional love."

Messiah Seed 9
To Love is to Free

Messiah, know that you cannot 'fix' or 'save' any other. To think you can is to attempt to separate your Self from a judgment, that is really about your Self, and to project it outwards onto another. You are not here to 'be saved' or to 'save' anyone else. If you wish to aid another, then know that the only way to fully do this is to love them unconditionally. It is in the experience of unconditional, universal love that *Self as God* is seen.

If your soul dream is to be a great spiritual master, then know that this is no more, and no less, than being one who loves all unconditionally, such that they may open themselves to the realization that they, too, are God. When such love is discovered, it is realized as the Self, for *you are love*. When you feel as one with all, then there is nothing but love for all. The spiritual master is one who purely realizes that they are love. There is no effort. There is no toil. There is no sacrifice. There is just love that radiates. Realize that there is no one great secret and, thereby, cease to search for that which, if known, would be the solution. There is no hidden solution. It is right in front of you in the art, literature, and many other diverse expressions of being, that have been recorded over the ages. You are love. *Be* love, and the reality that you seek will be yours.

Know what love is not. Realize that you are not loving another if your action limits or harms your own being. You are not loving someone if you sacrifice your own being for them. To make a sacrifice for another is to take away *their* power, *their* choice, and *their* right of creation. To sacrifice for another is to live someone else's life rather than your own. No matter what the short term benefits may seem, to sacrifice is to simply delay the moment when you will *take back* that power, to retrieve whatever it is you have sacrificed. Know that there is no dream, or wish of your soul, that exists to be sacrificed.

Know what love is: what it is to truly love someone. It is to desire, and act, to make them more *their* Self and not more *your* Self. It is to fuel and empower them, but not direct them. You are love. You are free. Free your love. *To love is to free.*

"I choose to live in joy."

Messiah Seed 10
No Thing Separates You from Joy

Messiah, know that the understanding of no one *thing* is necessary for joy. If you are feeling either joy or fear, then you are engaging your path. Understanding of how you are on your path is not required to experience the joy of your path. In life there is the constant choice of joy or fear. To manifest the choice for joy is to decide, with all your being, that you are ready for and deserve to feel joy. Everything before you on the plate of your life is there for a reason. Do not doubt this, for to do so is to live in a reality where you believe there are mistakes. There are no mistakes. If there is a morsel of food on the plate of your life that you do not like, eat it to find out why it is there and you will move beyond it. In this way you will make room for something new.

Know that there is nothing, *no thing*, more important or more spiritual than being in your joy. There is no spiritual ideal; no spiritual truth; no spiritual goal that requires you to sacrifice your joy.

To enter your joy you must put down your ideas of shame, guilt and original sin. You must put down your *feelings of need* for salvation, redemption and forgiveness. Know that no one died for your sins because there were no sins to die for. The Cross is but a symbol of the shame and guilt that humanity still carries. The Cross is something that each of you must put down of your own accord. To see Christ on the Cross is to see your Self as deserving of, or desiring of, crucifixion.

Do not do anything from an idea of it being for a 'higher purpose'. Do it because you feel to, because you want to. Then, and only then, will you be radiating the fulfillment of your soul purpose. Only then will you be living the legacy spoken of by the great spiritual masters, such as Jesus Christ, Buddha, Sri Krishna, and Lao-Tzu. If salvation exists, then it is the realization of joy and not death. You do not need to die. You do not need to be 'saved'. You need to live. Live in joy.

"I choose to live my dream in this lifetime."

Messiah Seed 11
Realize and Release Your Dream

Messiah, you are not alone. Do not fear that you are alone in your state of *being*, for you are not. Face your fears; face your Self. And, when you wake up, you will see that you are in a world of Messiahs, each with a purpose as grand and special as your own. Realize this so that you may step into the dream in your heart; your soul dream. Release the dream into your being and live it, for that is joy, and that is the experience of Heaven. Know that Heaven is a state of being within you; one that calls to be realized in *this* lifetime and not in some distant future.

Realize into reality what you feel it *can* be. Know that to truly realize something is to *release it into being*, and not merely to understand it intellectually. To realize something is to *be it*. Realization is not a state of intellectual truth; it is the *bringing into being* of your Light. To *know* is to *realize;* is to *feel;* is to *experience with all your being*. Feel what you experience with all your being and you will feel *All That You Are*, and that is God.

Know that the dream in your heart is there for only one reason: for you to live it and be *All That You Are*. It *is* possible to live the dream in your heart. To do so you must simply step out of your own way. The only thing that separates you from your dream is the belief that it is not possible. Know that your soul dream *is* possible and you will instantaneously start to experience it unfolding. Allow your Self to experience your dream unfolding.

"I choose to celebrate diversity."

Messiah Seed 12
Know You Are God

Messiah, know that to end suffering *you* must reach the feeling of your own worthiness and step into the fulfillment of your dream. *Realize* your dream into reality and *live* it. You must not only come to acknowledge your dream, but also reach the state of being where you *feel* your inner power to will it into *being*. Be your dream.

Realize, know and be *All That You Are*. This is to come to know that you *are* as God, and to not doubt that realization. This is the meaning, and its fulfillment is the creation of Heaven on Earth. Its fulfillment is that which all souls seek and can only come from within. The beauty is that, with this realization, that *you* are God, comes the realization that *All* are God. It is the path back to the Unity from within division, and *that* is God realizing, into *being*, the state of Unified Diversity. The unification of humanity will celebrate, not repress, its diversity. It can be realized no other way. Without acceptance of all, there is not complete acceptance of anything.

Unified Diversity is the evolution of the singular Messiah into *All as Messiah*. It is the realization of divinity as being *of the Self*, and not of some external deity. There is a God; an *All That Is*; a Tao and it is the source of all beings, all realities. You are 'it', experiencing itself in a state of limitation. So, from that perspective, you are more limited than it, but *you cannot be less* than it; for *you* are it, *choosing* to be in a state of perceived limitation. You make that choice each time that you choose to be born. You make that choice with infinite wisdom and purpose. Within the realization of that purpose lies your joy, for the result of that purpose *is* joy. The expression of joy is the expression of love. The expression of love is the acceptance of the moment. The acceptance of the moment is the acceptance of the Self.

Whatever your dream is, realize that to live it you must accept it as being your dream. Realize the ways in which you resist the acceptance of your dream. Realize the ways in which you judge your dream. Accept that your dream is your dream.

Messiah, accept your dream.

"I choose to take the conscious awareness of my worth into all situations."

Messiah Seed 13
Feel Your Worth

Messiah, know that to allow your Self your dream will take but one thing and that is to *deem your Self* worthy of it. All your life you have been told that you are not worthy of your dream. Know that is a lie that separates you from the full realization of your Godhood. Are you willing to allow your Self the realization that you are absolutely and uniquely special? Are you willing to actually *live* your dream, instead of just hoping for it? Are you willing to *give your Self* what you want? Are you ready to *admit to your Self* exactly what you *really* want?

You do not need to choose to experience pain in your expansion of being; but know that to walk your path you must face difficult questions, difficult answers, and *great change*. Know that you may have to let go of things you have previously used for feeling comfort and safety. In believing that these things kept you safe, you let into your *being* the illusion that you were in danger. You are not in danger.

To come to *value* your Self is to *come* to your Self. To come to feel your worth is to come to *be* of worth. All that you value in others, but not in your Self, is a symbol of your own worth that you have externalized. To come to your own worth is to draw back into your Self the power that you have given away. Realize that there is no need to prove your worth. To believe this is to believe that your worth lies in some act; an act you deem you must perform in order to prove your worth. Worthiness is a feeling and not an action. To allow that feeling into your Self is but a choice; the choice to see your being through eyes of love and acceptance.

Know that *you* determine your worth. If you feel any other has damaged your feeling of Self-worth, then know that you have the power to take that worth back. See whatever they said, or did, to you as the distortion that it is. Realize that you gave your power away by believing in that distortion. To feel your worth is to put down your baggage. You are ready to put down your baggage. You are worthy and always have been. You are a valuable being. *Feel your worth.*

"I choose to share the dream in my heart with others."

Messiah Seed 14
Be Your Dream

Messiah, know that you are unique. You are uniquely special. The paradox (the question and answer) that you contain is uniquely yours. The path to it is your dream and your dream is in your heart. To find your dream you must open your heart. To fully open your heart is to come to love your Self without reservation. The realization of your dream can only be manifest through that love for your Self; and, to love your Self, you must love *All That You Are*. To love and accept your Self is to discover that you are worthy of your dream. When you feel worthy of your dream, then you will have the courage to give it to your Self and, in doing so, *be All That You Are*.

Many are now waking up to the understanding that they are God and in this they may allow themselves to remember their dream. But what is a dream if it is not realized? It is a dangling carrot. So, do not just understand *how* you are God, but *be* the unique expression of God that *you are*. Be the fullest expression of the God that you chose to be when you birthed here. Be true to your Self. Be your true Self.

True realization is *being*. It does not mean 'to come to understand'; it means 'to bring into *being*'. To come to understand something is courageous and shows the willingness of the soul to expand. Beyond understanding is *being*. If you only keep your dream within the reality in your mind, then that is the only place it will exist. Realize that there is no facet of your mind that you cannot express out into reality and live. You only need to *believe* that you can. Start by verbalizing your dream. Words are a spell; when you speak them, so you create. Speak your dream and you will begin its manifestation. Begin to walk that path and you will see that you are in your joy. Joy is the realization of your dream, from the moment when you first conceive of it, to the moment when you *are* it. Joy is not for the future; joy is for *now*.

"I choose to experience my Self as who I am in the <u>Now</u> rather than through the idea of who I am based upon my past."

Messiah Seed 15
You Are Not Your Past

Messiah, realize that in each moment the Universe is created anew. Do not be afraid of the idea that in each moment you are just beginning, for in this understanding lies a great freedom. Know that the Universe was not created billions of years ago: it is being created *now*. To understand this is to realize that you exist in limitlessness. You are not constrained by what came before you. In each moment you recreate the Universe. Do so in a new and exciting way. In each moment you can start the creation of your dream out into reality. In each moment there is the potential for everything to change. In each moment everything changes. Every moment is equal.

Realize that it is not the past that determines your *now*, it is *you*. The degree to which your *now* comes to reflect and adhere to your past, is purely a representation of your belief that your past dictates your future. It is a common trap to perpetually recreate the pain of your past, by holding a belief in its power and focusing upon it. Until you stop the pain in your past from creating fear for your future, you will be stuck in a loop of reliving it. To break this cycle you must take your power back from the pain. Do this by allowing your Self to feel the pain totally. Allow it to make you stronger by taking back your power from it. Realize that, if you choose to carry pain from your past, then on some level you must believe that you need it. You do not *need* this pain. You do not need its limits anymore.

Just because your past was one way does not mean your future will be the same way, unless you *resign* your Self to that belief. Do not let your history of pain deter you. Take back your power from your past. Realize that your Self-doubt has created a tangible face in your reality. Go out and prove your Self-doubt wrong. *You are NOT your past*. To live in your past is to continually recreate it. If your mind constantly dwells in your past then open your Self back up to it so that you can fully experience and release it. Know that all things, once fully experienced, cease to perpetuate for they no longer hold any message for you. Your past is an idea that you can use to either empower or dis-empower your Self. Empower your Self through an empowered perception of your past.

"I choose to move towards my fears so that I may release their gifts of empowerment into my life."

Messiah Seed 16
Integration of Fear

Messiah, to realize *All That You Are* you must face your greatest fears. Know that your greatest fears all come from the fear of *realizing* your soul dream into reality. Between you, and the realization of your dream, is *nothing* but the *illusion* of your fears. Face the illusion. Face your fears. Rather than harming you, they will empower you. Fear is power given away that, when faced, will integrate back into your being, moving you closer to the conscious realization of *All That You Are*.

Fear of your dream is the idea that you are not worthy; not good enough, not strong enough, not deserving enough. Know that your fears are not to be resisted but embraced. They are signposts to your dream. You created your fears to hide your dream from your Self. Therefore, your fear is the exact thing that will lead you back to your dream. Fears are a trail of light that, when followed, will lead you to your *true* Self; the *limitless* Self that knows not fear.

Rejoice in the discovery of a new fear, for it means you are close to releasing it. Through that release you will experience an ever increasing freedom of *being*. Every fear is a limitation that, when undone, becomes a freedom. Fears are freedoms that you are denying your Self. Do not fear to be free.

Be careful not to create fears through your Self doubt. Realize that some fears are so old that they can be let go of just by the realization that they exist. The letting go of fear does not *need* to be painful, but sometimes you will insist on pain, in order to feel you have *worked* to overcome your fear. Sometimes you subconsciously ask for a fear releasing experience to be difficult in order to feel that the fear was 'justified'. See through these illusions and realize that fears can be dissolved by no more than your conscious intent and your resolve to integrate them. Do not struggle with fears; merely turn your attention to them and watch them disperse in the light emanating from your being. Set your intent and know the solution will come to you. If you *know* it will come, it will. *Life can be as easy as you are willing to believe it can be.*

"I choose to radiate joy."

Messiah Seed 17
Joy

Messiah, know that the process of realizing your dream is a path of pure joy. The living of your dream is your joy. Follow the light of your joy: *it is you in limitlessness.*

Joy, the thing the heart wants most, is your salvation. Do you understand this? To seek your dream is to seek your joy. The route to salvation is not a path of redemption. It does not require giving up the things you want and living in modest subservience. It does not lie in ritual and penance. It is not found in seeking God's forgiveness. The only forgiveness you need is *your own.* The route to 'salvation' is in allowing your Self all that your heart desires. The route to salvation is the living of your dream, and no soul dreams of suffering, of being caged, or becoming trapped in a belief in lack. The realization of all soul dreams comes from the realization that the Self is unlimited. Know that all seeming limitations are but Self-manifested illusions created by your fear of being *All That You Are.*

Do not fear that there is something selfish in seeking your joy because you see suffering in the world around you. Realize that the ending of suffering comes from the *living* of joy. As you come to live in joy so you will radiate that joy and, in doing so, aid others in finding their own. Your joy will connect you with the world and all beings in it. Your joy will make you more compassionate, not less. Realize that service to others will flow naturally from your joy, whether that service is direct or indirect. The attainment of your joy is not some 'perk' of reality. It is your responsibility to your Self if you wish to experience *All That You Are.*

Know that all states of being are naturally infectious. Realize that how you feel touches the people around you, whether you interact with them or not. You are a beacon of your being. Radiate joy. Radiate love. Radiate the Light that you *are.* Instill the world with your happiness and you will transform it a hundredfold more than if you radiate pity, sorrow, or anguish for the suffering of others.

The Messiah Seed

"I choose to feel happiness for the joy of others."

Messiah Seed 18
Be Happy for Others

Messiah, constantly seek to free your Self from the idea that the grass is greener on the other side of the hill. Realize how this belief has constantly drained your power and hindered you from fully realizing the wonder of *All That You Are*. This belief is to wish that you *are not* who you *are*; it is to believe that what you *are* is inferior to what you *could be*; it is to not like who you are. To like where you are, *like your Self*.

Realize that this archetypical energy, of wanting what you do not have, is the manifestation of your belief in lack. Put energy into it and the Universe will always validate that energy, showing you that love and joy are everywhere *except* where you stand. Allow your Self to want. Allow your Self to want *more*. Do this from a feeling of joy for what you want and not from a point of disrespecting or diminishing what you have. With the power of your feeling of joy you will manifest your heart's desire. Realize that you can accept what you have with your heart and still want more; but do this from living in the acceptance of your Self as you are, and not from the *want* for what is yet to come. *Love your now.*

Through this understanding, learn the power of being happy for others where *they are*, without it causing you to want to be where they are. You will find that, when you are truly happy for others, you will share in their happiness in ways you did not realize were possible. To envy others is only to harm your Self, for the joy of others will become pain to you. You will come to surround your Self with misery in order to not feel that pain. In doing so, you will disconnect your Self from the realization of the joy within you. To see joy in another and be angry that it is not *your* joy, is the choice to live in anger and not joy. Realize that this choice is *always* yours.

Know that to be happy when good things happen to others is to share in their happiness and that, to be envious of another, is to separate your Self from your *own* happiness. *Choose happiness.*

"I choose to serve the All through living in my joy."

Messiah Seed 19
The Nature of Service

Messiah, each time you move towards *being* your dream, any suffering created by you *not being* your dream is released from the world. Know that, as you move towards your dream, you are constantly aiding every other being in existence through your process. Do not *try* to be of service to others purely out of the belief that it is a 'good' thing to do. To do that is to hold a belief in right and wrong. The concept of right and wrong is an illusion; it is religion; it is dogma. Instead, know that by walking your path, you are *naturally* of service to others. You need not *try*. You need not force it. Service to others is love and love cannot be forced.

Realize that the highest service you can bring to this world is in *being* your dream. This does not mean that you do not offer a hand where you can. Know, however, that the best way to help people to live *their* dream is by the living of *your own*. Do not let being of service to others prevent you from *being* your dream, for to do so would be to diminish your Self and, likewise, all creation. Find a balance and learn the power to say 'no'. Realize that you may have to overcome your fears of rejection and abandonment to do this. Free your Self from these fears. Put down that baggage from your past and then *love* will radiate from you, rather than *need*.

Do not walk your path for the inclusion of, or to the exclusion of, *anyone* else. Feel in your heart when to help another and when to refrain. Do not judge this feeling or apply the morality of society to it. No matter how good your intentions are, if you act against the heart when it says "No", then you will often prolong another's suffering. To serve without *living* your Self is to be a slave. To truly live is to serve *all*, in every moment, without being a slave to any. In your many lifetimes you have all been slaves. You do not need to feel guilty in this life for not being one. Beyond genetic heritage is a spiritual heritage that knows no division. You have been every color, every gender, every sexuality, every *everything*. As you come to know this, the lines that separate you will come to dissolve and you will see the Unity that you *are*. There is nowhere you have not been. You are God.

"I choose to create space and time in which to experience the gifts of my life."

Messiah Seed 20
Know Your Fears

Messiah, know that fears are cages that you have used to limit your Self. As you face each of your fears, so you will go through a continual process of freeing your Self from cages; cages that you previously could not name, but have always felt. Fears are cages within cages, mazes within mazes, and must be faced to experience your Godhood in ever expanding ways.

As you come out of one cage, you will most likely find your Self within another. Realize this to be the encoded baggage of many lifetimes. Know that for each fear that you face and overcome you will reap rewards. With each bond released you will become more and more fulfilled; more and more the God that *you are*. Celebrate each victory of your spirit. Allow your Self to enjoy the rewards, rather than ploughing into the next challenge before you have had time to rest or to experience the joy of the victory. The rewards of life are not forced upon you. You must pause and focus on them to experience them. To do this is to love your Self. Enjoy the challenges you so love, but also allow space to enjoy the rewards.

Do not become discouraged by the amount of cages you must free your Self from. To do so is to focus on the destination and to not enjoy the journey. Learning to embrace the journey is essential for joy. The more you love your life, the faster its magic will unfold. As you learn to move with the changes that the resolution of fear brings, so you will lower your resistance to the journey; the resistance that causes you pain. You are here to *enjoy* this journey and not to suffer through it. The only proof of this is in the living of it.

The letting go of continuity may feel like you are entering chaos. At such times, center your Self and become the calm eye of the hurricane, knowing that you will not suffer unless you allow your Self to fall into fear. Know that you are the master of your fear and, *for this reason*, you will not fall into fear. You do not *have* to suffer, no matter what is happening around you. Your fears are illusions and you will come to see through them. Know your fears and they will not be fears, at their root is usually resistance to change. *Fear is no more and no less than the unknown.*

"I choose to release all preconceptions
of how my dream will unfold."

Messiah Seed 21
Let Go of the How

Messiah, when calling your dream into reality, do not presume to know *how* it will come. Many of your dreams may initially *appear* to be impossible. If you give into this belief, then they *will* be impossible for the duration of that belief. Realize that not knowing *how* it will happen is a limit of your comprehension and not a limit of the power of the Universe. You do not need to know *how* your dream will be possible for it to be possible. You must simply believe that it *is* possible. In this way, learn not to limit the creational powers of your spirit.

By thinking you must know the 'how', you develop the belief that your dream could only come to you in a certain way. To believe this is to severely limit the options by which your spirit can deliver your dream into realization. Focus on your dream and *feel* it into being, without attachment to how it manifests. Through imagination, experience the joyous feeling of living your dream, with total belief that you *can* live it, and you will draw it to you.

Realize that simply *thinking* it will happen will not make it happen. You must *feel* it with *all* your being and that means surrender, the facing of fear, and the letting go of the limiting beliefs in which you have cloaked your identity. Start with what you *can* believe, what you *can* accept, and work outwards. In this way, you will come to realize how much it has only ever been *you* that has hindered the manifestation of your dream. The conditions of your reality are only ever the manifestation, and not the cause, of the state of realization of your dream. This is the taking of responsibility for your Self. Have the courage to face the cynic and pessimist in your Self; that voice which you tend to call the realist. Know that it is the idea of being a 'realist' that has taken away your hope, out of the fear that having hope will hurt you. For many, this may mean facing their own judgment of what they perceive as naivety.

Dream with the heart of an infant; a child that has not yet been taught by society how to limit its options. Remember the state of being where you once dwelt; where anything was possible. Know that *anything* is possible.

"I choose to see that the Universe always supports me."

Messiah Seed 22
How the Universe Supports You

Messiah, realize that the obstacles to living your dream are all of your own creation. Know that the Universe never acts to hinder or limit you. Realize the truth that the universe is only ever saying to you, "How much will *you let* me give to you?" Accept this *one* idea and *everything* will change.

Know the Universe is your ally and will aid you whenever *you* allow it to. Realize that its power to aid you is *only* limited by your beliefs about what is and what is not possible. In each moment, reality is but a mirror of your beliefs, reflecting back to you what you believe. Face the reality that the only thing you have ever been fighting for is to come to love your Self. Realize that when you have been caught up in the chase of becoming, in the chase of trying to make your reality acceptable to your Self, then you have been fighting to accept your state of being. Beyond acceptability is joy.

If your reality seems bleak and limited, it is only because the Universe is trying to show you that some of your beliefs are bleak and limited. It does this with total love, so that you may change those beliefs and be free of them. Know the perspective from which *you are your reality*. If you work to transform your *Self*, then you will change your reality. If you work to transform your *reality*, then you will change your Self. Do not buy into the belief that your reality is a prison in which you must live. It is a canvas and you are the painter. Reality is a *being*; a loving being, that is continually showing *you* to your *Self*. Many of you have forgotten this and, instead of changing what you do not like, you resign your Self to it and unknowingly choose suffering.

Reality is a mechanism of the Universe which supports you by unquestioningly proving to you that your beliefs are true. Realize how your beliefs form your reality. If you feel your worthiness, and believe in your dream, then the Universe *will* give it to you. Know that if you feel unworthy of your dream, then reality has *no choice* but to confirm that unworthiness and deny you your dream. Realize the perspective from which reality is your servant and not your master.

"I choose to experience my body as being a living expression of my consciousness."

Messiah Seed 23
Love Your Body

Messiah, do not see your body as a limitation, for it is not. Your body is only, at any moment, what you believe it to be. If you believe your body is degrading, then so it is. If you believe that your body is healthy, then so it is. If you are ill, then realize that the illness has purpose. Feel the purpose and allow the illness to transform your consciousness. Know that *everything* in your reality is a teacher. Learn what it has to tell you and it will transform.

Feel that your body is a part of your consciousness, but understand that it also has its own consciousness. You cannot, therefore, disregard your body and expect it to live through your mind. It is a part of you that needs to be loved, and integrated, like every other part. Love your body and it will serve you well. Mistreat your body and it will let you know, because you will be mistreating your Self. As with all things it is a question of finding the *balance* that is right for *you*.

If you perceive your body to be a limitation, know that once free of it, outside of physicality, you will remember it as a unique and treasured experience. How much better would it be to appreciate your body *now* rather than waiting until it dies before you realize this? Know your body. Love your body. Accept it as a part of your consciousness, your spirit. Know it is meaningful and not an obstacle to be transcended. It is chosen. You chose it with purpose.

Know the balance between treating your body well in the physical and loving your body with your spirit. Realize how these are really the same thing. Treat your body like an old car, that constantly needs a kick-start, and that is what it will be. Treat your body as an amazing creation of your unlimited consciousness and *that* is what your body will be. The choice is yours. The power is yours. Your body is yours and no *body* else's.

"I choose to give my Self as much time as
I need to make any decision."

Messiah Seed 24
Give Your Self Time

Messiah, realize that the greatest gift you can give your Self, when you are in difficulty with any decision, is *time*. If you have not come to a clear decision then do not proceed. If there *appear* to be time pressures on a situation, understand that you are the one creating them, and *deselect* them. *Will* your Self the time you need to make any decision. Know that time is a construct which the Universe uses to describe your state of being to you. Lack of time is a *feeling*. It is a feeling of lack.

Realize that to allow your Self time is to acknowledge and honor your Self. To make a decision in haste is to then live in fear that the decision was made incorrectly. This fear will affect the outcome. Do not, therefore, make decisions until you have reached a point in your Self where you feel confident in your decision. To have confidence in your decision is to lead your Self to the desired outcome with confidence. To not grant your Self the time you need is a form of giving away your power. At its root is the idea that you are in a system that has the right to dictate your actions to you. It is to believe that there is a force that you must defer to in making your decisions, even when you do not feel ready.

In the moment where you allow your Self time, *feel* that the answer to your decision will be revealed to you. Feel the answer ahead of you, moving towards you. Know that in just giving your Self the time, *and therefore space,* to make the decision, you will instantly give your Self the clarity that you seek. This is a form of allowance. Allow your Self the time you need. It is a gift of *energy* to your Self.

A Messiah, whilst seeing through the illusion of time, still uses time for as long as it is useful. Know that no decision is forever. You can always change your mind. Release into your being the power of changing your mind. Change your mind. Speak your mind. Speak the change that you represent. All beings represent a journey of change, and to deny that change is to deny your Self.

"I choose to experience the limitlessness of my will."

Messiah Seed 25
Free Your Will

Messiah, know that there are an infinite number of ways in which you can move into limitlessness. Just as you can create what you *do* want, you can also deselect that which you *do not* want. Realize that when you say 'no' to something which appears in your reality, you do not need to consciously see *how* it should come to not be so. Do not be attached to the means by which you deselect your manifestation. To do so is to limit the ability of your spirit to remove the manifestation. Simply, with your heart, *will* it to be gone. Realize the perspective from which limitlessness can be described as the understanding that *there is nothing in reality that you cannot say 'no' to*. To experience your limitlessness you must face your fears, but there is no one way in which you must do this.

There may be many manifestations in your reality that you perceive as being negative. Know that through this simple process you can remove them and thereby bring your Self to a more joyous world. Realize that to deselect something, that holds a message for you, will cause it to re-manifest in a different form. As you come to see your reality with clarity, you will learn which aspects are simply historic relics of fear that can be quickly removed, and which are current lessons to be gone into. In saying 'no' to a current lesson, you will simply create a new vessel for the message. Allow your Self this flexibility. If you do not understand the lesson in its current form, then use your power to change it. In this way you can free your Self from the perceptually negative history that can collect around a lesson you are resisting.

Know that you are not a slave to any element of your reality, unless you *choose* to be. You are tied to nothing, not one aspect of your reality, through anything but your beliefs. So if you make bonds, rather than making them with fear, make them with love and joy. Realize that to be a slave to an element of your reality is not a 'bad' thing. It may well serve you on your journey for a period of time. Just remember, and *own*, that it is always *your choice*. Your reality is the product of your beliefs incarnate. You are the experience of your beliefs incarnate. You are the power of your beliefs. You are the power that ultimately chooses your beliefs. You are the power of a freed will. Free your Self from the constraints you have placed upon your will.

"Through my inner trust for my life I choose to embrace the unfolding of my future."

Messiah Seed 26
Do Not Fear the Future

Messiah, do not give your power to the future by fearing it. Realize each moment to be a product of your belief system, your energy, your motivation, your intent, and your inner feeling for your being and life. Realize that you have spent your life creating your Self. Have faith in your Self. Know that whatever happens was created by you, to be the *best thing* in that moment, for your journey to limitlessness. You are the carrier of your own message. Listen to your message. Listen to your Self.

Know that every moment that arrives is a moment that you have spent a lifetime honing to perfection. Realize that *All That You Are* has sculpted these moments from an understanding that is currently beyond your own and, therefore, have a deep faith in the events that unfold, as to do this is to have a deep faith in your *Self*.

Realize into consciousness the perspective from which you do not need to fear, as what will be will be. This does *not* mean that your future is predetermined. What it means is that nothing, no thing, is a mistake. All is with purpose. All is with meaning. All is of value. To understand this is to not fear the future. To realize this is to embrace the future as being the unfolding of your own limitlessness.

If you fear the future, then you do not fully trust your Self, your spirit, or your life. It is true that fear has come from your past. It is true that you can list many times when things went wrong. Realize that the belief that those perceptually negative manifestations will unavoidably recur creates an energy that feeds into the creation of your future. It is a Self-perpetuating belief. Accept and integrate your past. Realize its purpose. Integrate its lessons. Do this and you will free your future from being your past *relived*. Do this and you will realize that you do not need to fear your future. You will come to consciously create it with your love, and not subconsciously with your fear. Do this and you will collapse the future, and the past, into the *now*. You will be without regret for the past, or fear for the future. To live anywhere but in the *now* is to live outside of your Self. Have the courage to live fearlessly in the now.

"I choose to see through the illusion of external power."

Messiah Seed 27
External Power

Messiah, be free from the idea of blame. Realize that to blame another for *any* event or situation in your life is to enter into a state of delusion. Know that reality is a constant reflection of *your Self*. Any obstacles you find in your reality are but manifestations of blockages and fears in you, no matter how much another may *appear* to be creating them. Know all else, all others, as your teachers, for even a person blocking you is another Messiah showing you to your Self. See that all abusers and victims are in a dance together, one seeking to take power and the other seeking to give it away. The lesson for both is the same. It is for each of them to stand in their own power. Abusers seek power, from a fear that they lack it, and victims give away their power, from a fear of what they will do with it or what it will do to them.

Know that when either victim or abuser stands in the recognition of their own power, then the cycle of abuse and suffering ends. From this perspective, do not see an abuser or a victim as being different. To see them differently is to feed into their belief that they are different, when in truth they are one. In this way, a Messiah realizes never to take sides, for to do so is to reinforce the creation of division where there is none. All conflict is created by the seeking of power or the denial of power. All participants in conflict are seeking to find their own inner power. If it is not played out, it will not resolve. If it is quelled it will re-manifest. If one side is destroyed, another side will come up to take its place.

Know that all external power is an illusion; a contradiction. There can never be an ultimate external power. Power is not external. Realize that you are each inviolate; belief in external power is a denial of this. To try to control anything except your Self is to be out of control *inside of your Self*. Take control of your own being, live in your own inner power, and the need to control others will leave you. If you do this, you will *free* unimaginable amounts of your energy, which you can then put into the manifestation of your dream. Do not seek to control abusers or victims; *love them or leave them alone.*

"I choose to experience my Self as being the only true source of judgment that resides over me."

Messiah Seed 28
Self Judgment

Messiah, know that in order to become your dream you must become the ultimate decision maker in your own life. This is to say that you must step into your power. Come to realize that you are the ultimate creator of your reality and, as such, you are the highest level judge of what *you* do. Do not defer your power to choose to *any* other entity, physical or non-physical. Listen to all that you feel to and then decide for *your* Self. Know that the only true judge of any decision is the heart. Even if you do not follow your heart, and you fall into suffering, do not then allow that to burden you when you re-enter the stream of your heart. Learn from the experience and let it go. Let go of regret, for to have regret is to be in a limited view of your unlimited Self.

Know that there is *nothing* above you judging you. You are in a reality of total free will. Letting go of judgment of Self, as being a factor in your decision making process, can *only* come from you. *No other* can make you take your own power. There is no higher authority to which you can give your power, unless you create the idea of one in your own mind, in order to limit your Self. This has been strongly manifest in the idea of God being external. It is the externalization of your own power. Realize that giving away power comes primarily from Self judgment. Many of you have come to judge your Self and, in doing so, you have externalized your own divinity and set it up above you; looking down on you; being in judgment of you. What you may fear as the judgment of God is but the Universe's reflection of *your* judgment of *your Self*. Cease to judge your Self and you will integrate into your being the wonder that you perceive as being an external God. Rest assured you will still love God! This is the discovery, and not the loss, of God.

To know you are God is to know you are all one being. To know your Self as God is to know *all* as God. To know your Self as God is to know no potential outside of your Self that you do not contain. You are the miracle of your own beingness. You contain the infinite potential of expression of all that can be imagined.

"I choose to flow effortlessly with the currents of my life, knowing that they will always take me towards All That I Am."

Messiah Seed 29
Let Go

Messiah, know that *All That You Are* is constantly helping you as much as you will allow it to. Know that to move forward there will be moments when you must *consciously* choose to open new avenues in your life. Realize also that there are times to *sit back* and allow *All That You Are* the room to manifest magic in your life. All trust and faith can ultimately only stem from the Self.

Have trust and faith in *All That You Are* to weave new strands of possibility into your life. Create space in your heart, mind and beingness to let this happen. Allow your spirit space in which to move. Know that *All That You Are* can create the *how* of what your heart desires, in ways you could not imagine. Realize that by letting go of the tight reign you may have put on your life that you are not loosing control, but are exercising the greatest trust and faith in your Self. You are saying that you trust the currents of your life to carry you, by whatever means they choose, to a destination that was especially created for you. It is to trust your *being* to help you consciously be *All That You Are*. It is to know you are surrounded by love and support from the Universe, from God, from your very *being*.

Allow your life room to breathe. If you impose your *will* on every aspect of your life, in an attempt to totally control your experience, then your spirit has no room in which to maneuver. Realize that the greatest learning often stems from letting go and seeing what happens next. Life is a teacher. When you do not know the answer, just *let go* and let your life speak to you. It may take you to a beautiful new location beyond your dreams, or it may take you to unresolved pain. Know that, wherever you end up, it is where you best need to be in order to embrace the full experience of limitlessness. Thank your Self for this gift. Give the gift of 'letting go' to your Self.

"I choose to share my success with others and to feel the success of others inside of my Self."

Messiah Seed 30
Division

Messiah, when all beings come to love, then *All* will become a Unified Diversity. Realize that, in leading up to this point, the medium of physicality will become more and more permeable, for matter is primarily manifest as a symbol of division. With this permeability you will come to transform and manipulate matter in new ways.

Each struggle in your life is a representation of not feeling *as one* within your Self. Just as loving your Self is the same as loving the world, so it is with the journey to feel *unified* in your own being. The breaking down of division, in both the external world and your internal Self, occurs through love. When you come to love a part of your Self that you previously did not, then it becomes unified in your manifestation of the world. By your nature you separate off, within your Self, that which you are uncomfortable with. Loving your Self is therefore about breaking down internal division. In a parallel way, you label and segregate elements in the external world that you are uncomfortable with. These are purely symbolic representations of the parts of *you* that you are uncomfortable with. It is the world as a mirror of your Self.

When you break down a division in your view of the world, you will have broken it down inside of your Self. Similarly, if you work on a prejudice internally, when you have resolved it, you will find that you no longer see its counterpart in your immediate reality. Know that when you act to resolve a division in your Self then you will aid all others who carry that division to resolve it inside of their own Self. You are a mirror of the whole, and every *personal* breakthrough is a breakthrough for the *whole*. Every success in the world is to be celebrated. Know that when you come to feel the success of others as your own, so you will come to your own success.

In many ways, you are already unified, both individually and collectively; it is just that you must bring this unification into your state of realization. There is no effort. There is no unity that you must work together to forge. It already exists. You must merely open your eyes to it in order to exist in it.

"I choose to experience any hatred that I feel for others as the realization that I am not accepting an aspect of my Self."

Messiah Seed 31
Hatred

Messiah, see hate clearly. Do not attack people who hate, even though at one level, this is what they are asking you to do. Hate is essentially a cry for help. It is the manifestation of internal division. Know that it is impossible to hate anyone more than you hate the most rejected part of your Self. Hatred for others is an externalization of internal Self-hatred.

What you hate is a symbol of what it is *in you* that you are not accepting. Realize that you will need to look beyond the surface in such matters. Some hate anything that they see as representing change, as they do not wish to change themselves. Some hate anything that they perceive as being weak, as they hate their own weakness; they fear vulnerability. Some hate all authority, as they fear their own power. Some hate anything feminine, as they do not accept their own femininity. Some simply fear anything that is different from them, as they feel no security in what they are. Whatever it is that is hated, know that to hate something is to announce that you are *of it*. It is to say that it contains something *that is in you* which you are either rejecting or denying. When a person hates, they are in fear and to be in fear is to be in pain. Hatred is Self-mutilation. Do not, however, fall into thinking that it is wrong. It is not wrong to hate. To think it is wrong is to hate hate.

Do not curb your hatred simply because you may be rejected for expressing it, as that would be to contract into fear, and the reason why you hate would not be touched upon. It would just be buried beneath more fear and pain. Do not hate hate. To shine love on hatred is to reveal its root so that it may be healed. It is to provide a space for the person to see, for themselves, that they are in pain, so that they may recognize it and release it from the world. To say that you only hate hate is to say that you still hate, and that you hate that you hate. Hating hate may seem 'moral', but realize that this judgment only compounds the hatred and keeps you trapped in the cycle. Hating hate does not work towards ending hate, though it is a valid stepping stone on the path. If what you want is for people to stop hating, then you must love them. If you cannot do this, then just *leave them alone* and look at your Self instead.

"I choose to give love to my Self, knowing that in doing so I will radiate that love into the world."

Messiah Seed 32
Love Your Self

Messiah, when you are standing at a crossroads in your life, realize that the greatest block that you can put in front of your Self is the idea that there is a 'right' choice. The idea of right and wrong has long been a foundation of existence in your reality and, therefore, there is much that you may find needs to be unwoven to let go of this belief. It permeates all things.

When you are making a decision, use the opportunity to observe the origin of the thoughts that you have. Are you listening to your heart? Are you listening to society, your parents or friends? Are you listening to your own internal concept of right and wrong? Are you listening to what you believe would make you a 'good' person? Are you looking to fulfill the needs of others and ignoring your own needs? Know what informs your decisions. Know what forms your decisions.

Learning to observe your mind, whilst you are standing on the point of freewill, will teach you much about the psychological baggage that you carry. It is to come to see the filters through which you are creating your reality.

Realize that only when you give your Self love *first* can you truly radiate love. Only then can you fully create space for others to fill themselves with love. Make your choices from your heart, without fear that this is selfish. The love of the Universe is bountiful and your heart is of that love. At times, it will ask you to stand in front of others to fill its own cup and, at other times, it will ask you to act with total altruism. Trust that whatever it tells you is best and for the benefit of all, even when it tells you to put your Self before others. Realize that love for Self is the foundation of love for all. See the perspective from which love for *Self* builds love for *all*; and, conversely, how love for *all* can be used as a denial of love for Self. Love for all, without love for Self, is running; running from what you feel your Self to be, no matter how noble it feels. All freeing choices start with love for the Self.

"I choose to know my judgments as being of my Self and not of others."

Messiah Seed 33
Judgment

Messiah, realize that to all beliefs the Universe simply says 'And So It Is'. In doing so it reflects back to you what *you* believe. Know that you can consciously be the master of your beliefs. You choose what you believe. Do this according to your heart and not your reason. Only *you* have the power to learn to act from your heart and not from your fear, hurt, or conditioning. Realize that you use *reason* and *logic* to disguise these feelings, concealing them both from your Self and from others.

With the realization of the power of *Self* over belief comes the understanding of the redundancy of judgment. To judge another painfully is to experience the pain that the judgment represents manifest in your own life. This simply means that you will live within the experience of your own judgment. Realize that to judge another is to seek to externalize your own pain, under the illusion that it is being carried by someone else. Know that this is not wrong. It is the way of the reality you have chosen to exist in. Realize that beyond judgment is love. Judge and you will live in a reality of beings that you feel separated from. Love and you will live in a reality of beings that you feel close to. To come to that love is to come to cease to judge your Self. To cease to judge your Self is to see your Self, and the world, in clarity. It is to see your unity with all other beings.

Know that you cannot help but judge. What you then *do* with your judgment is the choice. Use it to see your Self and you will move into an ever expanding freedom. Deny your part in it and you fall into the trap of living in externalized pain. Realize that, if you judge others, then you will come to be surrounded by those very people, until you acknowledge that the pain which they represent lies within your own being. This is *not* the Universe punishing you; it is the Universe *loving* you. It is your life trying to end your suffering by showing you any pain that you are carrying. Your judgments are messages of your unresolved pain. Instead of feeling guilty for any judgmental feelings you may have, use them to free your Self.

"Knowing that it does not serve me, I choose to release the act of worrying from my life."

Messiah Seed 34
Do Not Worry

Messiah, know the difference between constructive problem solving and worrying. Worrying is an expression of fear. It has many colors, spanning from Self-punishment, to the thought that you must be a very noble person to worry so much.

Realize the perspective from which worrying is an intellectual extrapolation of a physical survival instinct that no longer serves you. See how the *act* of worrying is the giving of your energy to your fears and, as such, actually serves to manifest them rather than prevent them. To worry is to show that you are not trusting in your Self.

Know that to cease to worry is to release the *need to control* your reality. To cease to worry is to be confronted with your fear directly, rather than experiencing it through the guise of a worry that you have determined to be justified. To *will* your Self not to worry is a useful tool to identify and release fears. In the release of the process of worrying you are surrendering to the divine flow of your life and giving over trust to your *being*. This will release you into ever greater freedom.

Know that worrying is an expression of fear through which you try to control your reality from a perspective of pain avoidance. It is, therefore, to some extent coming to define your life and your choices from a definition of pain rather than joy. Worrying is currently the most pervasive form of fear expression and, if you give it your power, then that power will come to contain and limit you.

Realize that you have the power over which thoughts you give your energy to. Do not berate your Self for having worrying thoughts. When you identify them as such, simply let them go. If letting them go brings up a fear, then work with that fear directly, and not on its manifestation as worry. Free your mind from worry. Do not fear that to not worry is to live in delusion or idealism. To not worry is to live in total inner trust, joy, and love. Choose *spontaneous being*, not worry. Choose *love*, not fear. Worrying is not constructive problem solving. Worrying solves nothing.

"I choose to acknowledge all time constraints
as being of my own creation."

Messiah Seed 35
No Race

Messiah, as you open your Self to change, realize that reality is not a race. There is no ticking cosmic clock. Know that to feel under time pressure is a form of giving away your power. To think you are fighting against the clock is to live in a fear that you may not arrive 'in time'. Realize that there is no 'in time' to arrive in. You can arrive at *any* time, or you can arrive from outside of time. You will arrive when you arrive and when you arrive will be perfect. To arrive, and then anxiously check the clock, is to instantly knock your being out of the *now* moment into a state of Self judgment.

You are a master of time and you can even create extra time when you need it. In any moment, the concept of your being *against* time will instantly take you into a reality where you are facing an opponent; against whom you may either win or loose. Let go of this concept of time and you can only win. If you enjoy the jeopardy created by racing, then enjoy it; but do so with the understanding that, if it starts to cause you worry, then you can stop and take *your* time. You have the power to do this.

Know that being open to change is no more about being open to huge amounts of change than it is about being open to small amounts. Realize that it is not about quantity. Sometimes a giant leap is what will bring you into the greatest appreciation of beauty. Sometimes just the *finest adjustment* will unleash the greatest freedom. Quantity is an illusion. See both the fine and large adjustments that will lead you to your joy and limitlessness.

You are not in a competition with any other being, for you are *all* beings. Any concept of a *race* is created by your Self, to be against your Self, even if that is disguised in an externalized form. The feeling of jeopardy and adrenalin may be desirable to you for a while. Know that if ever that *rush* turns to fear, you can cease the race. Appreciate the perfection of the *now* and know that the next moment will be just as perfect *whenever* you arrive at it. Transcend the boundaries of time by allowing time.

"I choose to fully experience my pain so that I may release it from my life."

Messiah Seed 36
Positive and Negative

Messiah, make your choices in life from a point of view of selecting joy rather than coming from a place of pain avoidance. At one level, this is the same as saying love peace rather than hate war. It is to say define by the positive and not the negative. To free your Self from judgment enough to do this is to transform your reality into being defined from positivity rather than from negativity. Realize that this is not about denying negativity, for all things in your life are there to be looked at. It is, instead, about looking at the negative from a positive perspective. To do so is to see how to transform the negative into positive. If you need to feel pain, then feel pain; but do not elongate it into suffering by coming to define your Self by it. Allow, forgive, release. Allow. Forgive. Release.

Feel and release your pain. Realize that this can be a beautiful experience. It is only when you either come to define your Self by that pain, or become attached to it from the desire of expressing the victim role, that pain becomes suffering and that is a burden that does not need to be carried. Guilt and shame are the two emotionally expressed *beliefs* that most elongate suffering.

Look at your beliefs about any pain you are feeling. See if those beliefs are aiding the release of that pain, or if they are holding it to you. If you feel pain as anger, then express it as anger. Know that wherever that anger takes you, or anyone else, is where *you* and *they* are, for a good reason, choosing to be. To judge your own anger is to deny the experience you have chosen. To deny anger is to deny a part of your Self and live in separation from *All That You Are*.

Love and anger are not incompatible. Angry feelings can be expressed completely in love. Allow your Self to express any anger that you feel in order to assert your boundaries and feeling of Self. Realize that anger does not need to attack but, even if it does, if that is how it bursts out, have faith in your Self that you are creating an experience that will be for the benefit of all involved. *Trust in the expression of your life.*

"I choose to release the concept of right and wrong."

Messiah Seed 37
Right and Wrong

Messiah, free your Self from the concept of right and wrong and the more subtle, insidious concept of better and worse. Know that the idea of right and wrong is not something intrinsic to your reality but is, instead, something that you overlay onto your perception of it.

When reality presents you with a choice, and you are not clear on which road to take, do not get caught up in believing that there *must* be a right and a wrong path. Free your Self from the idea that one decision will be better than the other. To think in such terms is to create a reality where you are in jeopardy; where choices are tests and, depending on your answer, you will be led to either a good or a bad consequence. Realize that this is not how it needs to be. It is only *you* that makes it feel like this when you assign labels of right and wrong to your choices. Know that to free your Self from this is to exist in a reality that is a rose without thorns. Reality is not, by its nature, a negative experience. Know that you assign meaning to reality and not the other way around.

When you are faced with a choice that you find difficult, think of all options as leading to positive outcomes. Imagine all outcomes as joyful, see how they are different, and select whichever one *you* want *based upon* the feeling in your heart and *not* upon the logic of your mind. Once you decide, feel joy and confidence *in* your decision and, thereby, do not give your power away to doubt or fear *of* your decision. Know that there is no decision that can either save or damn you. In a world without the belief in good and evil, there is neither salvation nor damnation, there is only *being*.

Allow your faith in your state of being to free you from the need to judge your Self or the choices that you make. Know that there is no such thing as a mistake. Feel totally free in the consideration of all options presented by your choices. You are totally free. Your *will* would not be truly free if wrong existed. Know you have *free* will.

"I choose to shine my light unashamedly."

Messiah Seed 38
Shine Your Light

Messiah, inside of you is Light. To express this Light is to embrace your divinity. To hide from this Light is to hide from your divinity. Shine dear one. Do not be afraid to stand out in the expression of your Light. Do not be afraid to be different, even though in past lives this may have led you to suffering. This is no longer the case. History does not need to repeat itself. If you can release your roots that lie in fear, and embrace the change that shining your Light will bring, then that Light will bring you joy. Know with all your being that it can only ever bring you joy and it will be so.

Do not be afraid to shine. You say, 'Who am I to shine?' You say, 'We are all one; therefore I cannot stand out as being different.' You fear the world will tear you down for being so presumptuous and arrogant as to shine. This is a redirected fear of your Light, much of which may be stored in the very cells of your body from your childhood or past lives. Enter your body fully and exist in it; *feel* love in it and you will release these cellular memories.

It is through the shining of your Light that you will *all* connect together as one. Shining your difference is what will unify you, both internally and externally. What, at first, made you feel different will be that which makes you realize that you are one. Through the embracing of your alienation comes Unity. Know that *in* the Light you will discover the experience of 'all as being of one'. Become one. Live in harmony. Live in a Unified Diversity. Do not fear. Do not fear your Self. Do not fear your Light. It is that which is carried eternal. It is the Godhood that you currently deny. Do not deny your Light. Do not deny your Self. Do not deny the existence of God. To feel God is to feel your Self. Shine your Light. Shine bright. Shine *unashamedly*.

"I choose to take responsibility for all my own suffering."

Messiah Seed 39
Suffering

Messiah, know that to be *All That You Are* is to stand in your power of choice. It is to come to the realization that you have ultimately been the one who has created all the suffering in all of your lives. Realize that this idea may take some integrating. Allow your Self time to do this. Do not try to go faster than your own personal speed of assimilation.

To know that you created all your own suffering, combined with the realization that you are all one, is to know that you created suffering. You have, at certain points in your life, represented the choice to suffer. You have chosen suffering. If you are suffering now, then you are choosing suffering. Allow your Self to feel angry. Realize that, as scary as this concept feels and as angry as it may make you, allowing this feeling is the ultimate doorway out of suffering. To realize that you have created all your own suffering is to then realize that you have the power to deselect it, just as you had the power to choose it. Know that to deselect something is to simply stop choosing it. To stop choosing it you must first acknowledge that it was *you* who chose it originally.

Know that no matter how much you have raged for your suffering, no matter how much you have cursed existence, you do not need to be forgiven. To feel anger at your own suffering is a part of the process of taking your power back from it. If you still feel the need for forgiveness, then forgive your Self. It is not wrong to suffer. You did not do anything wrong. The idea, that to suffer you must have done something wrong, was a point of view adopted to try and make the idea of suffering acceptable. It then became a tool to control, used predominantly by organized religion. Release your concepts of fault and blame and you will see what suffering is. Accept the right of others to suffer.

Do not fear suffering. Do not fear anything. Do not choose to simply 'not suffer'. Life is far more than 'not suffering'. Life is joy. Life is freedom. Choose freedom.

"I choose to know my Self as the determinant of all jeopardy in my life."

Messiah Seed 40
Jeopardy

Messiah, realize the perspective from which life is like a movie that is constantly creating itself; the idea that you are in a movie which you are watching. Know that you are as physically safe as when you are watching a movie. From the level of your spirit there is no jeopardy. All jeopardy is an illusion. You are in an illusion that allows *you* to create the illusion of jeopardy.

Realize that, as much as you like to feel safe, you often like to feel in jeopardy. The enjoyment you derive from experiencing jeopardy is why you sometimes go deep into the illusion that you are separate from God. Know the level from which you enjoy jeopardy, so you may better choose when you do, and do not, want an experience to go into jeopardy.

Know that you are now, if you desire, exiting jeopardy. We are here to greet you into reality without jeopardy. Know that you are totally safe at all times. You are immortal. Realize immortality as safety. You are safe. Know that nothing external can touch the God spark that you are. All you previously considered as jeopardy is but the creation of attachment. Realize that attachment creates jeopardy. Know that attachment is not wrong. To want to experience jeopardy is not wrong. Know when you are choosing jeopardy. Know and own the attachments that you have. Take ownership for all the jeopardy in your life by knowing that you created it. Take responsibility for your own drama.

Recognize that to experience jeopardy, you must forget this understanding of what jeopardy is. Through this, realize how your mind can switch what it does and does not remember, in order for you to experience any state of being that you desire. Enjoy jeopardy, because you are safe. *Feel safe.* Jeopardy is but an option you choose to express your fear. Allow it to reveal, rather than cloak, your fear.

"I choose to realize the ways in which
I fear my own being."

Messiah Seed 41
Fear of Limitlessness

Messiah, understand that as wonderful as limitlessness sounds, there *are* ways in which you fear it. Know the perspective from which it can be said that you must fear it, as otherwise you would be living it. You will know when you are in limitlessness for, in that eternal moment, you will be living your dream.

Realize that limitlessness is frightening in that to be in a state of limitlessness is to be in a state of unlimited possibility. This is a state where anything, *any thing,* can potentially happen. It is this infinite potential that anything can happen, at any moment, which is a root fear for beings in your reality. It is the pure antithesis of consistency. As you move towards limitlessness you will need to overcome your inclination to have reality be consistent.

Realize how the need for consistency points to the nature of fear; namely why you fear fear. Know that to fear something is to give it energy. To give something energy is to fuel its state of manifestation. This is how you create what you fear. Therefore, in a state of limitlessness, where all is *instantaneously* possible, a fear is instantly made manifest in every detail. Your being knows this and, as long as it knows fear then your being will fear limitlessness. In limitlessness, to fall into fear is to live in the manifestation of that fear, just as to be in joy is to instantly be in an expression of Heaven. To be in limitlessness you cannot fear your Self. Fear is that which knocks you out of the conscious experience of limitlessness.

In this way, the Messiah overcomes the thought that if all that it took to be happy was being happy, then surely everyone would do it; the reasons why people choose limitation over freedom become clearer. To release your limitations is to release your fears. Your fears are your limitations. Release them and you will enter the full conscious experience of *All That You Are.*

"I choose to experience all perceived rules as being personal choices and not universal laws."

Messiah Seed 42
No Rules

Messiah, realize that the ideas and laws that appear to govern your existence do not define you; *you define them*. Scientists seek to study and reveal the laws that underlie the natural world. They seek to uncover how the hand of God created reality, and they hope to see through to the divine order of *All That Is*. What they do not realize is that they are *creating* these so called laws *as* they discover them. Through the *expectation* of their belief and through the decisions with which they create their measuring devices, they predetermine what it *is* that they believe they are objectively measuring.

Reality is a unique projection created by each of you. You each contain *all reality* and have the ability to intersect your personal realities to create a seamless mass reality. *All That You Are* is encoded into your reality and so it can be said that the scientist is exploring what *they are*, using their external manifestation of reality. Know there is no right or wrong in how you experience your *beingness*. The methods of the scientist are as valid as that of the overtly spiritual. Realize that you are *not* on a spiritual quest *discovering* what you are. Instead, just like the scientist, you are *creating* what you are. What *you are* is not written in stone with you on a quest to reveal it. What you are is what you *choose to be* and, in exploring states of being, you further come to refine what it is that *you are choosing to be*.

Realize this and you will be starting to grasp how exciting limitlessness is. *There are no rules*. You are making them up as you go along. Realize that you probably fear that you are 'making up' the rules as you go along. This fear is the fear of the realization that *anything* is possible. You fear *anything* being possible. To your Self-limited mind this unlimited idea can feel like chaos. You are in fear that you are truly the creator of your reality. Know that the greatest joy lies in embracing this idea. To come to know that you create your reality is to create your dream, as that will be the first thing you create when you unleash your Self upon the world, and that is when you unleash the world of your dream upon your Self.

"I choose to open my heart to feel acceptance for all things."

Messiah Seed 43
Acceptance

Messiah, realize the joy in acceptance. Acceptance is a state of *heart*, not of mind or matter. Realize that to accept another is *always* to accept a gift. You are each a gift. To fully accept a gift, and experience its joy, let it into your heart. Realize that the route to joy lies through the heart. *Accept* the gifts of your heart.

Many of you feel guilty when you receive, because you do not deem your Self worthy of it. Sometimes, upon receiving a gift, your reaction is to instantly think of what you can give in return that will be of equal or greater value. That is not accepting a gift. Until you come to value your Self, you will not be able to receive into your heart and you will find your Self separated from the love and joy both within and around you. Realize that to value your Self is to accept your being. To value your Self is to experience the gift of your being. There is little joy to be derived from the world if you do not accept your Self first. It is to live a life that you do not accept, in a reality that you do not accept, from a state of being that you do not accept. It is to live in denial of your Self. *Do not deny your Self.*

Feel that acceptance is a state of *open heart*. Know that all acceptance leads to the joy of feeling the Unity of all life. You cannot accept another more than you accept your Self. To value another, more than you value your Self, is to love your Self in the guise of another. What you love about the other in this state is but a quality in your Self that you are not *feeling* inside of your being. Conversely, know that what you feel hate for in another is but a quality of your Self that you are not accepting.

Know that all hate stems from lack of acceptance. Realize that you *can* choose not to be something that you accept. Support the rights of others, even if they do not *seem* applicable to you. To accept something does not mean you have to *be* it. A positive choice does not need to infer the existence of a negative choice. You can accept that which you are not choosing to be. Accept through the allowance of love in your heart.

"Through experiencing my Self as a Self-determined being, I choose to determine my reality with love and joy."

Messiah Seed 44
Self-Determination

Messiah, realize that as much as you are here to discover your Self, it is also true to say that you are here to *determine* your Self. There is no right or wrong in what you determine your Self to be, for there is only *being*. Know that you are Self-determined. Release into your being the power of your Self-determination.

Know that, as true as it is to say that to be Self-determined is to inspire positive action, so it is true to say that to realize you are Self-determined is to let go of control. Self-determination is also the realization that the invisible force you feel behind your life, that guides you, is you. To know you are Self-determined is to feel your Self in the touch of God. It is to see your hand in every miracle that you experience. It is to know your Self as the source of your own joy.

To feel Self-determination is to be standing in your own power. To be Self-determined is to know your Self as the final and most powerful force, in the personal reality that you experience. God has no desire to control you. Your free will to choose your reality is the trump card that beats all others, for that is what your reality is. This is the reality you chose to enter. It is not to say that you are the most powerful force in *the universe*; it is to say you are the most powerful force in *your universe*. This gives insight into the illusional nature of the concept of hierarchy.

Know that *you* are the determinant of your reality. Determine your reality with love and joy, and you will live in love and joy. Determine your reality with fear, lack and suffering, and you will live in fear, lack and suffering. Realize that the source of your determination is your *feeling* for life. Look at how you feel for your life. Determine how you want to feel for your life. See how your choices have created any discrepancy. Exercise Self-determination. Transform your reality into love, acceptance, joy, Self-empowerment, and allowance for *All That There Is*.

"I choose to assign meaning to reality that empowers my Self and others."

Messiah Seed 45
Meaning of Imperfection

Messiah, realize that imperfection and limitlessness are compatible. Imperfection does not limit you. Imperfection is a fundamental building block of freedom; that is to say *choice*. Freedom *is* choice. Choice *is* freedom. Being alive is *being* free to choose. *You are alive.*

Here is the central paradox of your existence - you are being asked to simultaneously realize that you are both perfect and imperfect, that you are infinite and yet limited, that you are God and yet human. Accept that you are limitless. Accept that you are imperfect. See the key. The key is that through accepting your imperfections you become limitless. Do not waste your life in pursuit of a perfection that already exists within your imperfection.

Know the power of acceptance. When you accept an imperfection in your Self then it ceases to be an imperfection. To accept an imperfection is to realize how it is perfect. What you perceive as imperfect *is* imperfect and will affect you as such. What you perceive as perfect *is* perfect and your interaction with it will be perfection. See how acceptance is a tool with which you can transform your reality.

Know that acceptance is a choice. *You* are the one that chooses what you do and do not accept. Even whilst you are trapped in limited beliefs as to what you can physically affect in your world, know that you are *not* limited in how you *perceive* it. Through the power of the *choice of your perception* you can live in whatever world you wish. What is being spoken of here is not a life lived in madness or delusion. It does not refer to a disengagement from the consensus reality. You will still perceive the consensus reality. What will be changing is the *meaning* that you assign to it. To change the meaning that you assign is to totally change any aspect of your reality that you desire to change. Know that reality does not come with pre-assigned meaning. No meaning is ever implicit, even though at times the consensus view can be so strong that it feels that way. Know that you do not derive meaning from reality, but that you assign meaning to it. Own and use that inner power.

"I choose to view reality through clarity
and not personal agenda."

Messiah Seed 46
Know That You Know

Messiah, to wake up to the nature of reality is to come to *know* that you *know*, whatever it is that you want to know. *Know you know.* *Feel* you know. Although you cannot currently house omnipotence in your physically manifest form, you *do* have access to omnipotence. You can know anything that you allow your Self to know, as long as it does not violate the freewill of another. Realize, through this, *the power of intention.* If your intention for what you desire to know is an attempt to violate another (which is to not stand in your own power) then you cannot know. *To know* you must stand in your own power. *To know* anything you must know your Self. As you come to know things of your Self, then you come to know of the world. As you come to know of the world, you come to know of your Self.

To not know your Self is to not truly know the world, for you are not able to differentiate your Self from it. That which you do not know of your Self you transpose onto your perception of reality or, phrased another way, that which you do not know of your Self you view reality through. This you most commonly call projection. You view reality through that which you are denying in your Self.

To know reality, know your Self. To know your Self truly, you cannot view your Self with an agenda of what you want to see. Realize that you *can* be anything, but to become anything you must first come to know what you are currently. To change any aspect of your Self, you must first know it. To know something is to be it. You must be what you *are* in order to be something else. The portal to infinite choice is *being* who you are. To be who you are is to allow the potential to be anything. Through Self awareness, singularities realize into being their own limitlessness. Through Self-awareness, and Self-acceptance of what you currently perceive as limited, you release that limitation back into the limitlessness from which it birthed.

"I choose to know my Self as being That Which Chooses."

Messiah Seed 47
That Which Chooses

Messiah, know your Self as *That Which Chooses*. What you *are* is *That Which Chooses*. You are the act of choice. You *are* choice. You are a product of all the choices you have ever made, and yet you are not any *one* choice. You can choose to undo all choices you have made, for in each moment you choose anew. You are the choice to choose. Within the Unity, the idea of differentiation and choice birthed as one. That idea was the first choosing of choice. It chose itself to exist. It cannot really be said whether the choice created the differentiation (limitation) or whether differentiation created choice, for they are one and the same. To choose is an act of differentiation. When you express a preference you come to further define what you are. You come to define your Self through your choices. Your very Self-definition is a choice which you are making in each moment.

Choosing in and of itself does not create limitation. It is that to choose you must be in limitation; you must be within that which can be differentiated into a choice. To do this you must be in a reality that includes the experience of Self and other. Therefore, you must leave the Unity to have choice. Having left the Unity, you desire to recreate the joy and harmony of the Unity, whilst maintaining choice. You seek to create Heaven on Earth. You seek *limitlessness* with choice. The Unity is limitlessness, without any choice, except the right to leave the Unity in order to experience choice. You seek Unified Diversity. You seek to not be alone; to experience the Unity whilst creating your own unique *being* through choice.

Know that through your choices you have the power to both unify and divide. The key to Heaven on Earth is to create Unity through the honoring of all diversity. Accept diversity. Accept your Self. Know that to accept your Self is to accept others and that to accept the diversity in others is to accept the diversity in your Self. You *are* a Unified Diversity. To realize your reality as a Unified Diversity come to realize your Self as a Unified Diversity. You are many expressed as one. Allow the paradox of experiencing the many in such a way that they can be experienced as being unified whilst being simultaneously differentiated.

"I choose to experience every aspect of my reality as being something that I have chosen."

Messiah Seed 48
Accept Your Choices

Messiah, to change your reality you must become aware, *at the level* from which you are choosing, of the element in your reality that you wish to change. You must become aware of the *original* choice that you made. Come to know why you initially chose what you now do not want in order to change it. Know that you have concealed many of the choices you have made from your Self.

To know why you made any particular choice can best be approached by first taking responsibility for that choice. Do this by coming to accept that it was *you* who made the choice. You cannot change a choice that you do not take responsibility for, as the act of not taking responsibility externalizes that power from you. As long as you refuse to believe that you could have chosen a particular element of your reality, then you are separating your Self from the knowledge of *why* you chose it. You are, in this condition, living in a state of denial and have little hope of changing the choice, except to change its form to another that you must then still deal with.

Know that to not accept an element of your reality is to not accept one of your choices. It is to not accept an element of your Self. To deny your reality is to deny your choices; it is to deny your Self. Realize that you do not need to feel joy for every element of your reality, but you must accept that it was *you* who created it. Through the power of acceptance comes the power to change. This could be described as the ultimate 'Catch 22', as it means that you must accept what you do not want in order to change it to something that you do want. Lack of acceptance is a separation of your Self from your power to choose. To not accept is to deny your choice of reality. All non-acceptance is reality reflecting your denial back to you.

Accept to transform. Transform your Self through the acceptance of your Self. Transform others through your acceptance of them. Transform your world through your acceptance and honoring of all that it contains. There is no thing that does not seek validation through acceptance. Know that the foundation of acceptance is love. All seek love.

"I choose to open my Self to experience my being in new and exciting ways."

Messiah Seed 49
Be New

Messiah, realize the way in which you both *are* God, and *are not* God. Imagine God as an ideal. You are not the ideal, but you *are* an expression of it in which the ideal exists *fully*, but in an encoded form. As you explore and develop the expression of your Self, so you decode the ideal into all that you express your Self to be.

Imagine God, the ideal, as being an open rose. You are the seed of that rose. You contain the complete awareness to transform your Self into the rose. There are an infinite number of ways in which you can do this; ways which, in this moment, you are creating with your *free* will. As you discover new and exciting ways of becoming the rose, so you *enhance* the rose; you enhance *All That Is*.

In this way, realize that you are God in a state of expressing and exploring the limitlessness of God. To be in a *state* of God does not mean to be *all* that God is, and yet there is no *state* of God that you are not free to explore. There is no part of God that you cannot be. Your choice is unlimited.

This is how you are both simultaneously limited and unlimited. This is how you are both God and not God. This is how you *are*. This is what allows you *to be*. This is why you should not seek to be All; you should seek to be *your Self*. The All already exists as the All. You are, however, the only being that exists as *you*. You are a totally unique and divine expression of the ideal. You are a birthing God. Do not destroy your Self to become what already exists. Be bold, be something *new*.

"I choose to be the conscious choice maker of my being."

Messiah Seed 50
The Choice of Your Self

Messiah, know that you, and all other beings, are an evolving experience. You are the experience of your Self, and you seek to enhance and diversify that experience. You are constantly sharing your experience; sharing what you are. The reality you experience flows from everything that you believe. You create your experience through your beliefs. You exist in the experience of your beliefs.

Know that, however it may seem, you do indeed choose your own beliefs. The responsibility for your beliefs is your own. In each moment you choose them and, in each moment, you can change them. Do not give the power of the choice of your beliefs to any other. To do so is to give them the power to choose your beliefs for you; that is until you choose to take back that power. Know that even if you give your power away, as completely as is possible, that the choice to take back your power remains with you.

If you are not willing to make choices in your life, then there are others who will make your choices for you. Realize that this occurs by default if you disregard your power of choice. Your world has a mass belief system. When you do not make a choice, then it is made from the mass belief. So, instead of owning your individuality, you take your choice of experience from the mass. This occurs with degrees of localization; with the beliefs of beings close to you, and the ideological groups you belong to, affecting you more than beings with whom you have a less direct association. Realize that this process occurs predominantly below the level of manifestation, meaning that the beliefs of those around you affect your choices, without that affect being perceptible on the physical level.

Know that although you have free will it is up to *you* to use it. Become aware of the choices in your life. Elevate your Self to the position where you *know* you are the one who has to make those choices, and then make those choices consciously and willfully. You are the choice of your Self. Become aware of that and take responsibility for it. Choose from *your* Self, and not from the mass. As you come to choose with love, so you will put that love into the mass belief system that affects all 'non-choosers' by default. To choose love for your Self is to feed love to the whole world.

"I choose to know my Self as a perfect expression of limitlessness."

Messiah Seed 51
Limitation and Limitlessness

Messiah, remember that the purpose of this reality is to *create* and *be*. If you feel that there *must* be a direction, then call it 'coming to limitlessness', which is saying 'coming to not choose limitation'. To some degree this can be seen as the idea that was translated into the concept of good and evil. That concept, however, has been taken somewhere more limited than the original limitation it was designed to protect people from. It is a tool of control that takes power through the promotion of fear.

Limitation is against the nature of the soul and leads to suffering. Therefore, to seek the expression of limitlessness is to seek joy. Limitation can produce suffering, as it is a distorted illusion that in some ways makes you *experience your Self* as being less than you are. Limitation acts to perceptually separate you from the limitless joy of your being.

You entered reality to realize and express *All That You Are*. The reward is the indelible joy that is written upon your soul. It is the experience of unlimited freedom, and that is experienced in a unique and powerful way when realized from within a reality that is defined by limitation. This is circular, with no beginning and no ending. As true as it is to say that God created your reality, it is likewise true to say that your reality created itself. Even in limitation you are a perfect expression of limitlessness. Even in limitlessness there is expansion. The resolution of this paradox is the resolution of all paradoxes; it is to realize that *you are God* and that *All is God*.

The circularity of paradox points to the root unity and harmony that exists within *All That Is*. As you come to realize limitlessness in limitation, so the circle will become a spiral and a new dimension of being is released into realization. Your reality will seem to continue as it is and yet everything will have changed. The ascension that you seek is not a defined event, it is already happening. Everything is changing, and yet, somehow, it seems to remain the same. This is *waking up*.

"I choose to experience my choices as being perfect for all."

Messiah Seed 52
All

Messiah, know that the mass shared dream can only be realized by your own realization and living of *your* soul dream. This is the case, no matter what your soul dream is, even if on the surface it appears that your dream is at odds with the mass. *Realize* that your dream fits perfectly into the mass dream. As you start to live your dream, so you will start to see its part in the overall harmony and motion of the All. You are harmonious with the All, whether you can see it or not.

Know that even those that appear to be purely of service to themselves are being of service to the All. The distinction of service to Self and service to others is an illusion. All service is service to the All. All action is an action for the All. All love is love for the All. All hate is hate for the All. *All all is for the All.*

To see this is to see that you are free and in a state of limitlessness. To see this is to be without restriction. To see this is to be free from fear. It is to know that all action is right action. Let go of the 'what ifs' for they are hypothetical projections and not reality. *Look at your now.* Look at the choices on your plate in this moment and know that you can make whatever decisions you want. Realize that, whatever you decide, will be perfect for *All* and not *just* for you. Embrace this freedom and know that, even if at this point you are not yet ready to act, then that is right action also.

Realize that just as the deepest desires stem from the desire for limitlessness, so the root of all fear is fear of freedom. In limitlessness there is no plan, no God to rule over you; no necessity for consistency and no direction that is best to follow. There is only your will, and from your will you form all that you experience. Trust your Self to give your Self love and know that all will be loved by that love; all will be freer as a result of *your* freedom.

"I choose to acknowledge my Self as being the author of my own life script, possessing the power to change it however I please."

Messiah Seed 53
Meant

Messiah, discover the infinite freedom that lies in the realization that there is no choice that you are *meant* to make in a certain way. There *is no meant*. There is nothing in your life that you were *meant* to do. There is nothing in life that you were *predestined* to do. There may, indeed, have been things you scripted to do, in the timelessness before birth, but do not extrapolate this to conclude that you are *meant* to do them. They are simply ideas that you felt would be fulfilling to explore. You can explore them in this lifetime, in another lifetime, or never.

If you wish to think in terms of some Master Plan that you are meant to follow then realize that, in each moment, that plan is being adapted and that *you* are the one adapting it. For most, to think of a 'Master Plan' is to desire the idea that there is some external force which has written a play that you are acting in. It is to want to divorce the Self from the feeling of the immediacy, the vibrancy, and the unpredictability of life. It is to not want to have to make your own choices, but to have a life that is prewritten for you.

Know that, with the realization that nothing is *meant* to happen, there is no loss of purpose or drive. See that any plan you feel inside of your Self *is* your own plan and, as the author, *you* can change it however you so desire. The signature on the inner plan of your life is that of God, and as *you* rewrite it so *you* will re-sign it.

In this life you are here to be what *you* want to be. If you must think of God as external, then realize that the only plan that God has for you is to realize, feel, and *be* whatever it is that you want to be. That is your exploration of *All That You Are*. That is to come to the realization that you are God. Truth is no more or no less than being true to your Self. The Will of God is for you to have your own will, and to use it.

"I choose to unleash the power of my imagination into the experience of my Self."

Messiah Seed 54
The Idea of Your Self

Messiah, remember that in any moment you are in a state of definition. You are *the idea of your Self* and you have total control over that idea. It is only through Self-imposed restrictions, on what you allow your Self to believe, that you limit what you can be. In this way, it can be said that you define your Self through limitation, for this is what your reality is. It is the medium in which that can occur. It is a medium that allows an infinite being to experience itself in a finite form and, that is to say, it is a medium that allows a limitless being to experience itself in limitation / separation.

You are not *becoming, All That You Are,* as you already *are, All That You Are.* You are simply remembering what that is. You are on a journey from limitation to limitlessness and, as you take this journey, so you are discovering *new ways* in which you are limitless. God can be seen as being the evolving concept of limitlessness. God *is* unlimited and is on the infinite path of discovering all the ways in which it is limitless. This is the paradox of how something can be perfect and yet evolving. Allow paradox.

You are a Self-aware, Self-defining belief system that both 'is' itself and 'observes' itself. You are the experience of the Self-determined belief system that observes you. Your belief system is an evolving expression of how you are, and are not, limited. The only limits are what you will and will not *allow* your Self to believe. Your only limits are your imagination (which is unlimited) and your *belief in your Self* to manifest whatever you can imagine.

Wipe away your preconceptions of what your life is to be, and imagine anew. Whether you realize it or not, you are living in your imagination. You are that which you imagine your Self to be.

Messiah, imagine.

"I choose to open my Self to fully experience all that I feel."

Messiah Seed 55
Feel and Know

Messiah, realize that to know is to feel, and that to feel is to know. The separation of these two words represents your ideological separation of the logic of your mind and the emotions of your heart. Know the space of being where these are the same. Realize into your being the unity of your heart and mind. Unify your perception of reality. Know that all your senses, both those that are biologically visible and those that are currently biologically hidden, can be unified into one sense. To exercise your complete unified sense is to be an empath. It is to experience whatever you perceive *as itself*; it is to experience the *beingness* of whatever you focus your perception upon.

Feel what you know. Do not live in a mind of rules and logic. Logic is thought without feeling and can only reinterpret what you already know. Logic is a wonderful tool, but in using it, understand that without inspiration it is a vehicle without fuel. The mind, integrated with feeling, is wisdom. Wisdom is to feel knowing and to know feeling.

Know what you feel. Let your feelings flow through you without inhibition or Self judgment. You can ask questions *of* your feelings, for they will teach and guide you, but do not question the validity, value, or 'rightness' of your feelings. To do so is an attempt to not *feel* them. Whenever you try to *think* your feelings, instead of *feeling* them, you are accessing but a glimmer on the surface of their depth. Allow your Self to experience openly what you feel, and then you will *know* what you feel.

When you know what you feel there are no questions and whatever reality your feelings are steering you towards will manifest. When you know what you feel, then your feelings will never lead you astray. When you are not open with your Self about how you feel, then your *interpretation* of your feelings will lead you to a reality where you will realize what it is that you are denying. If you feel freely, meaning without boundaries, then you will step from a cage that you may not even realize you have come to contain your Self within.

"I choose to face the realization that I can be <u>any</u> thing."

Messiah Seed 56
Be

Messiah, realize that to *know*, is to *feel*, is to *be*. To truly know something is to feel its beingness; it is to know what it is to *be* it; it is the realization of *knowing* into *being*. As you come to unify your perception and become an empath so you will enter limitlessness, as to *be* an empath is to have the ability to *be* anything. Realize that to be an empath is to be exercising your power of reality creation. It is, for that moment, to *create* the reality of another within your own being. To truly empathize with someone is to know what it is to *be* them, and that is to *be* what they *are* in the moment. It is to travel back to the Unity through the undoing of all choice and then to choose to be that which you wish to empathize with.

Initially you will experience their being within your own. As you come to trust in your Self, and your ability to not only transform your reality but also the expression of your Self within it, then you will be able to experience *anything* from *within its own being*. In this moment, you will experience directly the paradox of being your Self and yet being able to be all things. You will realize that there is no thing that you cannot be. There is no experience of *being* that you are denied. You are free to *be* anything.

To realize you can be *anything* is to start to realize what you are. When you can be anything, you realize that there is no one thing that is you. It is to know that you are *no* thing and, yet, have the potential to be *any* thing. It is to know Self as being *that which chooses* from a point of infinite choice. Beyond living the experience of your choices, you are *that which chooses* those choices. Travel into the core essence of your being and allow your Self to consciously experience the point of choice; the state of existence from which you choose. Go there. Be there. Feel this state as being alive inside of you. Feel this state as being you. You are *That Which Chooses*. Choose to know you have infinite choice. *Be* a living expression of infinite choice.

"I choose to feel any pain that I carry, so that
I may release the love that it denies me."

Messiah Seed 57
Pain

Messiah, realize that pain is not *inherent* to your *being* in any way. There is no pain that you are destined to live with, unless you so choose. Know the perspective from which all pain is love unexpressed; the denial of love in your Self. Realize that to love conditionally is to contain love unexpressed, for universal love is without limitation. You are universal love.

All existent pain *will* be expressed and to attempt to deny the pain within your Self is to force it into manifestation through alternate routes, such as your body. To release pain you must *feel* it. To feel pain is to travel into its core where you will always find love denied. It is only through your limitation of love that you can be hurt. To know universal love is to know no pain. To know pain is to not know an aspect of the universal love that you are. Realize that you are love in order to know no pain. Know your pain to come to know that you are love. Pain is your repression of the love that you are.

Love is limitlessness. Love exists in limitlessness. Hurt is love distorted into a limited expression. To end pain, know that you are limitless. You are love, and love has no limitations. Love with limitations is conditional love. Conditional love will manifest elements of pain as the representation of its limitations. To feel universal love is to feel love in an unlimited way; it is to experience love for all things, without differentiation. To feel universal love for another being is to love them without differentiation of their being. It is to love and accept them in their totality. Their totality is the potential to be all, just as that potential is yours. To love another in totality is to love your Self in totality; it is to love All in totality. Love another by allowing them to be whatever they choose to be. To love more is to remove restrictions from your love. To end pain, love more, not less. It is not love that has hurt you, it is *unrealized* love.

Let go of how you would 'like' love to be; what you *think* love should be. Realize that these preconceptions of love often stem from trying to protect and possess your attachments. Release these preconceptions of what love is and you will find love in all things. Be willing to see love in all things and all you will see is love. See with eyes of universal love and you will release the pain that you carry. To love is to transform your pain into love.

"I choose to experience my Self as pure love."

Messiah Seed 58
Love

Messiah, know that love is the answer. If love does not appear to be the answer, then realize that you are misperceiving love. Just as you cannot express limitlessness in words, so you cannot express love in words. Often you are left with realizing what is *not love* and that realization can ultimately lead you to discover what fear still exists in your being. Realize that all that is *not* love is fear and that to face your fears is to transform them into love. Know, therefore, that all is love. Fear is freedom denied. Love is freedom.

Realize that to perceive all as love is to perceive from a state of limitlessness. To perceive from limitlessness is to perceive from a state of infinite love, for limitlessness is love. To realize that what you *are* is love, is to come to perceive love in all things. To come to perceive your Self as love is to come to perceive the All as love, for you are the All and the All is love.

Realize that you will always see with the eyes through which you choose to look. You will always see what you look for, as what you look for is what you believe. Look with eyes of love and you will see love. As you come to realize into being the love inside of your Self, so you will come to see the love that surrounds you. To see with love is to transform your Self and your reality into *All That You Are*. To see love, you must believe in love. Believe in love.

Realize that love is a choice. You do not have to choose it. You do not have to choose limitlessness. Love cannot prove itself to you. Love is not there to break through to you. Love is not there to save you. Love cannot save you as there is nothing to be saved from. If you cannot believe that, then know that you can save your Self, from anything that you perceive a need to be saved from, simply through *being* love. Love is the answer to all things. To realize this is to come to realize what love truly is. To know what love truly is, is to become unlimited. To know love is to know your Self as God. You are the love of God. God is love. You are love. To know love, know your Self. To know your Self, love your Self. Love is the answer.

"I choose to know my Self as the creator of my reality."

Messiah Seed 59
You Define Reality

Messiah, realize that when it comes to reality, *you* define it; *it* does not define *you*. For many of you, the understanding of this statement, more than any other single thing, will free you into an ever expanding limitlessness. To truly understand it is to know that *you* are the creator of *your* Universe. It is to know your Self as God. *You are God.*

"I choose to embrace the unknown, including the entirely new ways of being that it contains."

Messiah Seed 60
Being Open

Messiah, realize that the seeming continuity and consensus view of reality is, on one hand, *the manifestation* of the harmony of the Unity from which you all birth *and*, on the other hand, it is *an illusion*. Know that you have given your mind the power to fill in any gaps in your experience, in order to cover over any discrepancies or anomalies that it may perceive. The purpose of your mind is to make sense of your experience and assign it meaning. Any information that it cannot handle tends to get passed over, with 'cannot handle' meaning that the mind is not able to assign an acceptable meaning to that information.

There are many other layers to reality and, as you come to develop your belief system to include more than is immediately apparent through the physical senses, so you will start to see these layers. Know that they are not hidden from you but that, through your choice of beliefs, it is *you* that has come to hide from *them*. This is often made manifest through either a fear of being insane or being perceived by others as being insane. To access these layers, you do not need any special knowledge. You do not even need to know what to expect. All you need is an open mind. An open mind is one that is curious and seeks what is unknown, instead of fearing it. An open mind *assigns space* for entirely new meaning instead of trying to make all experience fit into what is already known. An open mind *wills* itself to expand and change, rather than allowing itself to atrophy through a need for consistency.

Communicate with *All That You Are*. Be curious. Be open to change. Be open to new things. *Be open.* You may emulate a closed system as much as you desire but, in essence, know that you *are* an open system. All things flow through you, whether you acknowledge them or not. To be open is to choose choice. To choose choice is to choose change. To be open to change is to be open to the unfolding of *All That You Are*, for even when you express into reality *All That You Are*, you will always change, for *All That You Are* is an expression of change. This is to say that you are an evolving journey and not a destination. Being open to change is being open to your future.

"I choose to challenge the world with the love in my heart."

Messiah Seed 61
Challenge Reality

Messiah, do not believe everything that reality seems to be telling you. While it is true that reality is a reflection of your Self, you must equally understand that reality is also a reflection of the mass belief in limitation. Through your socialization, you have taken into your Self much that does not represent you. So when reality seems to say that what you want is not possible, do not believe it. Take up the challenge to prove reality wrong. Feel with your heart what is possible and act from that feeling. To learn to act from your heart, over what your other senses tell you, is to learn to *perceive* with your most powerful sense.

There is no bigger hindrance than the belief that something is not possible; the belief that 'it could never happen'. Do not doubt that *anything* is possible. If you want to do something that the world in general is not ready for, then you can still do it with those who *are* ready for it.

Recognize *no limits* and, through that, understand that even concepts like gravity are continually birthed from a belief in them. The speed of light was constant until someone conceived that it changes. In ways that seem impossible from within the illusion, the Earth was flat until someone conceived of it as a globe. To realize how this can be true is to let go of the idea of an objective reality and understand that reality is always just the idea of itself.

If your heart reveals a different message than the one that your physical reality seems to be presenting, do not be afraid to challenge your reality and manifest what is in your heart. To challenge reality is to challenge your Self. It is to break historical patterns that no longer serve you. Challenge reality with the love in your heart.

"I choose to experience my Self as being complete,
and as such, I love without need."

Messiah Seed 62
Universal Love

Messiah, do not fear love. Realize that to fear the hurt you experience when you lose something that you love, and are attached to, is to fear *attachment* and not love. Learn to distinguish the feeling of love and the feeling of attachment. See that you often blend these feelings together. Universal, unconditional love cannot be expressed through attachment. To love someone with conditions is to ultimately dis-empower, for it is to impose your values onto that person.

Realize that attachment is a form of giving your power away. To become attached to something is to believe that you would be *less than you are* without it. Know that neither the presence, nor the absence, of *anything* can make you more or less than *All That You Are*. If a person makes you feel closer to *All That You Are*, then they contain some aspect of your Self that you do not currently see as being *of* your Self. Love them unconditionally and you will come to see this aspect in your Self. If you try to possess them you will come to cage that aspect, which they represent, outside of your Self. Do this and you will enter into an endless chase to complete your Self, from a feeling that you are incomplete. Know that you are complete unto your Self.

Whatever it is in life that you want, or desire, then the answer is to love it without limitation. Know that every Self-created limitation of your love *will* be expressed as a barrier between you and what you love. Realize that this is to aid you in coming to remove those barriers, so that you may experience the love that you are in limitlessness and not limitation. To be in a state of attachment is to be in a distorted view of your Self.

Know that you can never fully touch anything that you are attached to, for you will always be experiencing it through the filter and barrier of your need; your feeling of incompleteness. To truly touch something is to love it without limitation. To love without limitation *know* that you are complete unto your Self. To love without limitation is to love without need. To love someone without needing them to be any particular way, is to empower them to be *All That They Are*. Universal love is universal empowerment.

"I choose to entrust my inner senses with total faith in their guidance."

Messiah Seed 63
Magical Senses

Messiah, realize that much of what you feel as being impulse, volition and intuition is, in fact, you tapping into the feeling of your future Self. Realize that, as you start to see through the illusion of linear time, so you will come to experience more of what you *have been*, and more of what you *will be*, all within the present. This is to say that you will come to experience more of *All That You Are* in the conscious *now*.

Realize that much of what you intuit is going to happen is, literally, a *looking into the future* through the loosening of the belief in *linear* time into *fluid* time. As you come to see how you are creating your reality, so you connect into *being* the God spark within you *from which you create*, instead of experiencing your Self as *what you create*. The closer you move to being *All That You Are*, the more you will start to experience its state of timelessness and non-definition. This will appear as the opening of your *inner senses*, those senses which are currently labeled as psychic.

Realize that, as real as these powers are, they are subject to your own belief system and that of the mass. This includes the use of your inner senses to prove to others that the inner senses exist. To tell someone of your inner experience, no matter how emphatic and persuasive you are, always gives them the freewill option to not believe you; to think that you are deluded or confused. The level of proof available for any phenomena is proportional to the allowance of the mass belief system for it. As the world comes to believe, so more proof will become available. Realize that this is purely referring to external consensus proof. Your inner senses can tell *you* anything, with a knowing *beyond* external proof, with that level of knowing being determined by the *validity* that *you give* to your inner senses. To learn to trust your inner senses is to learn to trust your Self.

Know your inner senses will grow as you come to both use and trust in them. Expand your *being* through inner feeling, not external proof, and you will embark on your own personal magical journey; a journey that will lead you to your magical Self. The allowance of magic is the allowance of experience, which is currently beyond your understanding, into your state of being. Know your Self as being magical and you will know magic within your reality.

"I choose to experience spontaneous being."

Messiah Seed 64
Self-Reflection and Spontaneity

Messiah, to know *All That You Are* is to realize that you are constantly meeting your Self. Do not presume that you know everything about who you are. Learn to meet your Self. To meet who you are in the moment, is to enter the next moment and then to turn and face your Self. Do not be afraid to observe your state of being. To learn to meet your Self is to come to be able to see your Self from a point of clarity and not from a point of seeing what you *want* to see. It is to view your Self without preconception.

Know that, after every change in your Self, you must meet that change. Changes are realized through choices. You will know you have changed when you see that you are making a different choice than you made previously. To know your Self, know *when* you are choosing, know *what* you are choosing, and know *why* you are choosing it. To become aware of choice is to become aware of your Self through reflection.

Know that Self-reflection in this way is a tool and not a necessity. When you come to be *All That You Are*, which is to say when you come to accept *All That You Are*, then you will come to live in *spontaneity* rather than in Self-reflection. In the experience of limitlessness, all experience appears spontaneously, as there are no boundaries of past or future; all exists in the now. Your birthing spontaneity will be the reflection of your birthing limitlessness. Self-reflection is therefore a tool that may aid you in the discovery of your own limitlessness but, in the moment of that discovery, it becomes obsolete. When you live entirely in the *now*, there is no past or future Self that you can look to in order to observe your Self.

Know that this simply means that you must first come to understand the definition of your Self, before you can then let go of that definition. Self-definition is a stepping stone to *no* definition. Limitlessness is simultaneously a state of *no definition*, a state of *ever changing definition*, and an expression of the equality of *all definition*. It is the *no choice* that is inherent in the realization of *all choice*. Treasure and use your volition; use it to become whatever you wish to be. Know that you must explore and realize definition in order to move into the non-definition of limitlessness.

The Messiah Seed

"I choose to let go of the need to control."

Messiah Seed 65
Letting Go of Control

Messiah, know when to let go of control and take your hands off of the steering wheel of your life. Do not do this from a position of testing God, or from anger at the Universe. Do not wait to do this until you are in a feeling of exasperation or last resort. Instead, let go with complete inner trust and confidence. To let go of control of your Self, and hand control up to the Universe, is to truly place your trust in your Self; and that is to know that you are the creator of your own life. It is to demonstrate that you feel the flow of life and know that it will take you where you need to go. It is to understand the level from which reality *can* flow, runs far deeper than your conscious thoughts. It is to believe that there are no external forces that can harm you, because you know that you are safe. It is to come to have released the need to create pain in your life, and to have realized that you do not need to clutch the steering wheel anymore, or watch every bend in the road for hidden obstacles.

If doing this brings up fears, then use this as an opportunity to see those fears for what they truly are. In doing so, they will evaporate and connect you further into your trust of Self, as both an incarnate being and as a spiritual presence that permeates all life. Realize that reality has a built in fail-safe mechanism to resolve any situation. That mechanism is simply *the letting go of control*. And, by using the word 'simply', it is to imply that it only requires the letting go of effort. But realize that the letting go of effort may, to start with, be one of the most exhausting things you have ever done, as your mind may initially feel adrift and frantic. Realize, therefore, that the need to be in control stems from a lack of inner trust.

Know that to be the choice maker in your life does not mean you should attempt to control every aspect of your reality. It can feel good to be in control; just do not *need* to be in control. To feel the *need* to control your life is to believe that your life would otherwise be *out of control*. Realize the illusionary nature of control. Make the choices that come to you and then let them go. Let them manifest their own resolution. Do not try to control the results of your choices. In this lies the resolution of the paradox of control of your life, being simultaneously absolute and yet totally illusionary. Make your choices and then let them go.

"I choose to experience the full spectrum of my being, from individual definition to unity consciousness."

Messiah Seed 66
Unity Consciousness and Individuality

Messiah, know that you are the birthing concept of Unified Diversity. You are the 'We in the I' and the 'I in the We'. You are the blending of Unity expression with individual conviction. You are conquering both the fear of Unity Consciousness (feared as being a state of 'hive mind') and the fear of Individuality (feared as standing *alone* in your state of being).

The conflict created by this paradox is manifest, at a mass level, as war. Fear of a unified consciousness with all other beings is expressed as territoriality, possessiveness and ownership. It is the fear that your *being* can be invaded. It is the fear of invasion. Fear of the power of any individual is fear of your own power. An individual can only come to appear to have external power when they have convinced others to give over their power. Know that no individual can have power over you unless it is you that is granting it. When you *know* war cannot touch you then it cannot. Honor the right of others to engage in war; do not give them your power by trying to prevent it. Accept the right of others to have war in order to come to live in a reality without war. Love peace. Do not hate or fear war.

Come to accept that you are an *Individual*. Know this as your power, as it means that you are the ultimate authority of your life, for *you* are the one that makes all of your own choices.

Come to accept that you are a part of *Unity Consciousness*. Know and feel that you are unified with All that is in your reality. Know that, as you awaken into Unity Consciousness with them, so you shall experience them and *All That They Are* directly, just as they will come to experience *All That You Are* directly.

Know there will be no secrets in the state of Unified Diversity. Come to accept your whole Self, for soon their will be no element of it that you can hide; not from others and not from your Self. Accept your Self to be accepted. Feel acceptance. Accept your Self in order to be *All That You Are* and feel unified with *All That Is*.

"I choose to allow my Self to know things, without needing to know how I came to know them."

Messiah Seed 67
Knowing Only What You Need

Messiah, realize that knowing is not an end result. It is not a state of acquisition of knowledge. Knowing is an *openness of being* to let in, and *be changed by*, whatever it is that you wish to know. Realize that if you will not accept the *change* that comes with a 'knowing', then you cannot know it. To *come to know* something is to *come to change*.

Through knowing, all things can be experienced *directly*, without the need for physical manifestation. Realize that this does not devalue physical experiences; they are totally valid expressions of 'coming to know'. For example, you have physically manifested this book into your life, thereby giving your Self a physically translated path that describes to you how you have come to know what you have discovered through reading it. Your mind is, therefore, kept happy by knowing *how* it came to know. This is how you use physical manifestation to give your mind a describable path of how you traveled from not knowing, to knowing. To move into an experience of more *direct* creation, start to allow your Self to know things *without* the physically manifest path. No physical experience is *required* to know the answers to your questions. Allow your Self to just know, without knowing *how* you know.

Realize that you *do* know what you *need* to know. To desire to know more than this is to choose to experience *denial of your limitlessness*. To focus on knowing something that you do not need to know is a way to distract your Self, and to remain in a circular loop of experiencing your Self as being limited. Focus on knowing only what you *need* to know and you *will* know it. Focus on knowing something else and you will be choosing to experience your Self in limitation. Allow not knowing what you *do not* need to know in order to fully experience the knowing of all that you *do* need to know.

To allow your Self to 'know without knowing how you came to know' is to realize that you have the ability to know *any* thing, in *any* moment, without *any* restriction. This is the realization into *being* of omnipotence. Your first experiences of omnipotence will be to know whatever you need to know whenever you need to know it. *Realize that this is the only omnipotence that you will ever need.*

"I choose to embrace and explore
all the facets of my being."

Messiah Seed 68
Masks and Facets

Messiah, realize that what you *outwardly* portray your Self as believing may not be what you really believe. What you *consciously* say you want may not be what you really want. How you *act* may tell a different story than what you *say*. Know that to say something is true does not make it true. What this means is that there is a disparity between what you are and what you project outwardly. Come to see this disparity. Do not judge the disparity that you find, but *do* see it, so that it may be a conscious choice and not a Self-deception.

You each play many different roles, with a different face for each role. Do not be afraid to look at the disparity in your life, for it is by seeing and naming the disparity that you can come to see what *is* you and what *is not* you. Through identifying your different masks you will come to better see your Self. Only by seeing your masks can you see with clarity the unified being that lies beneath them.

Know that masks are not wrong, for you are a multi-dimensional being with many facets. Realize the difference between when you are wearing a mask to distort your Self, and when you are wearing a mask to enhance and focus a particular aspect of your Self. Learn to embrace your faceted nature. Do not fall into believing that to be 'enlightened' is to become one consistent, ultimate state of being. Such a belief is a constraint on the exploration of *being*. Let your Self experience life in many ways, not in just one way. Your faceted nature is a part of the freedom of your being. Feel free to play different characters in the experience of your life. To say you are faceted is to say that you each have the ability to be anything that you wish to be, in any way that you wish to be it.

Know God as a diamond with an infinite number of facets. No one facet is God and yet each facet is an equal projection of the unified whole. Realize that a facet is a property of a diamond and, whilst being something unto itself, it cannot be separated from the whole. Know your Self as an evolving facet of God.

"I choose to experience the passage of time as being the continual unfolding of All That I Am."

Messiah Seed 69
Time as the Unfolding of Self

Messiah, know that what you perceive as linear time is the manifestation of your awakening to your Self. Becoming *All That You Are* is, from your perspective, becoming your future Self. Each moment you *awaken to* is a further unfolding of *All That You Are*. You are constantly moving towards *being* your future Self. Realize how the linear passage of time can be perceived as *an external manifestation of your becoming*. You are constantly moving towards the realization into being of *All That You Are*.

Let go of the notion that you can go backwards. It is impossible to go backwards as you are only ever experiencing more and more *being*. Through this, know that the unfolding of the future is the unfolding of your being. To realize this is to know that time is not something outside of you that you exist within, but that time is something which you create in order to further manifest the unfolding of your *being*. To know that you create *your own time* is to realize that the passage of time is not fixed. As you come to embrace change so you move into the future faster than if you resist change. Therefore, through your openness to change, it can be seen that you are in control of the rate at which you experience time. The objective measurement of time is only *one way* of perceiving it. Allow your Self to experience time in other ways. To view time as a series of seconds and minutes is like describing a landscape only in terms of acreage.

Time is that which allows the experience of becoming. You are becoming. The only thing between you and the conscious experience of *All That You Are* is the *symbol* of time. To realize that time is but a tool is to take power over the rate of unfolding of your Self. When you come to realize your power over time, you will come to realize that you have always been moving at a speed that is perfect for you. Know that all beings run at different speeds. What one person may experience in a day may take another person a year. To experience something at different speeds is to experience it with a different result. Faster is not better than slower; it is just different. Whether a being lives for days or years, at the end of their life they will have lived for a lifetime and experienced all that they wanted to experience in that form. Time is a facet of manifestation and not a framework into which manifestation must fit.

"I choose to exist in limitlessness."

Messiah Seed 70
Self Healing

I heal my Self through my acceptance of my Self. This book is an expression of my acceptance of *All That I Am*. I heal my Self through the realization of the love that I am. This book is an act of love. It is the purest expression of the light I experience within my soul that I have so far achieved. It is my greatest fear faced. The resolution of that fear is my realization of limitlessness.

I am human. I am perfectly imperfect. I am love. I am infinite. And so are you.

About the Author

Story Waters is a spiritual author seeking to empower people to discover and follow the divine light of their own being. He believes in the development of a personal spiritual connection free from the dogma and fear inherent in organized religion, feeling that many people have given away their personal power to society and religion instead of living what they feel inside of their heart. Through his writing Story hopes to inspire people to develop and follow their own inner voice, and to love and completely accept their own being.

Story was born in England in 1972. He studied Clinical Psychology for five years at university, but left one year short of obtaining his Doctorate knowing that it was not his path. He started channeling his wider-self at the age of twenty developing a powerful connection to his spirit in limitlessness. He quickly embraced the freedom of expression provided by the birthing internet to share his writing and digital artwork.

The Messiah Seeds contained in this book were written with Story drawing on over a decades worth of his notebooks revisited through his current state of awareness. Though Story still channels he no longer sees it as a distinct state but rather as an integral intuitive sixth sense as important as seeing or hearing. He is currently working on a re-expression of the classic Taoist text the 'Tao Te Ching' by Lao-Tzu as well as further Messiah Seed Volumes.

For further information please visit Story at Limitlessness.com.

Printed in the United States
22846LVS00003B/159